A TORONTO LAMPOON

Graham Pilsworth

A TORONTO LAMPOON

Edited by
Wayne Grigsby

Eden Press
Montréal · London

lampoon: a virulent or scurrilous satire (Oxford Dictionary)

A TORONTO LAMPOON
Edited by Wayne Grigsby

ISBN: 0-920792-38-3

© **1984 Eden Press**

Credits:
Original Cover Illustration: © 1984 Aislin
Book Cover Design: J.W. Stewart
Book Design: J.W. Stewart with Pamela Chichinskas
Illustrations: J.W. Stewart
Aislin cartoons courtesy of *TODAY MAGAZINE, THE MONTREAL GAZETTE,* and *TORONTO STAR.* Reprinted with permission of The Toronto Star Syndicate.
THOSE WERE THE DAYS by Allan Gould originally published in *KEY TO TORONTO,* March 1982.
Photo credits: Harold Ballard and Art Eggleton — CANAPRESS PHOTO SERVICE/*The Globe & Mail,* Toronto. Reprinted with permission.
GREAT GREASE and "Toronto police car" photographs by Russ Forfar.
RIGHT ORDER OF TORONTO and Ontario wine ad by Andrew Blanchard.
THE OFFICIAL TORONTO WORKOUT photographs by Jennifer Goddard.
LA VERA STORIA DI TORONTO photographs from M. Clark's grade 5 history project.
THE POSTLETHWAITE PAPERS photographs by Patrick Johnson.
We would like to thank the following models for appearing in this book: R.O.T. models: Peggy Bonspiel and Brian Goldberg. Grogan Quads: Zak Dutton, Gethin Stevens, Christopher Johnson and Julien Duchaine.
The publisher wishes to thank all of those who contributed to this effort. A special thank you to Christina Hartling.

Printed in Canada at Imprimerie Gagné Lteé.
Dépot légal — quatrième trimestre 1984
Bibliothèque nationale du Québec

Eden Press
4626 St. Catherine Street West
Montreal, Québec, Canada H3Z 1S3

Canadian Cataloguing in Publication Data

Main entry under title:
 A Toronto Lampoon

ISBN: 0-920792-38-3

1.   Toronto (Ont.)--Anecdotes, facetiae, satire,
etc.   I. Grigsby, Wayne

PN6178.C3T67   1984   971.3'541'00207   C84-090185-2

About the Contributors

WAYNE GRIGSBY is a Montrealer. (There, the secret's out.) And like most English-speaking Montrealers he has devoted a great deal of thought to Toronto: should he move or shouldn't he; is Commerce Court sexier than Place Ville Marie; could he live in a city where he'd have to take his career more seriously than lunch? A writer, broadcaster, critic and journalist, he has contributed to many of the national media. He likes Toronto. Really.

AISLIN is the pen-name of Terry Mosher. Originally from Ottawa, Mosher settled in Montreal, where he has been drawing cartoons ever since. Mosher has won a number of awards, including two Canadian Newspaper Awards, 1977 and 1978, the prestigious Quill Award, and five prizes from the International Salon of Cartoons. He is editor of *ZED . . . in Lieu of Canadian Humour*, a humour magazine making its debut April Fool's day, 1985. Mosher lives in Montreal with his wife, Carol, two daughters, one dog and eight cats.

LILLIAN ALLEN is one of Canada's nationally unknown poets. She moved from Spanish Town, Jamaica, in 1969. "I have these strange love affairs with cities," she says. "Thirteen years ago I moved to New York. I wanted to marry the city and have a baby. But I wanted an even keel and humane existence, so I came to Toronto in 1974. Since then, Toronto and I have developed this nice relationship, and now we're engaged."

RON BASE is the movie critic at the *Toronto Star*. He also co-authored the screenplay for *Heavenly Bodies,* coming soon to a theatre near you. He can hardly wait for the reviews.

IAN BROWN was born in a rickety house built on stilts over the raging waters of Lac St. Louis. Now he lives in Toronto and works as a features writer for *The Globe and Mail.* He is a partner in Invisible Books, a small publishing company in Toronto.

JOHN BURGESS was born in Hamilton nearly four decades ago. This is a handicap he has tried unsuccessfully to overcome all his life. He is a freelance writer and broadcaster currently living at City-TV doing entertainment for the late news. His hobby is resting on the sofa reading newspapers. He has next to no time for his hobby.

ELIZABETH CINELLO was born in Udine, Italy in 1958. She immigrated to Canada at six months old. The first few years were quite difficult, as she didn't speak the language and had no work experience. Canadian immigration officials were quite lenient, granting her Landed Immigrant status when they realized she posed no immediate threat to Canada.

DAVID COBB is a Toronto writer/columnist who sees a cliché when he knows one.

MICHAEL ENRIGHT is the editor of *Quest Magazine* and a broadcaster who lives in Toronto, and likes it.

KAREN FLANAGAN-McCARTHY lives in a trendy, renovated Victorian house in an untrendy ethnic neighbourhood, shops in Kensington Market and is not a member of 21 McGill. She works as a publicist for CBC-TV network current affairs department and as a freelance writer.

VICKI GABEREAU is a Vancouverite who moved to Toronto to advance her broadcasting career. Once the CBC gave her *Variety Tonight* to host, she moved back to Vancouver with her show tucked under her arm.

ALISON GORDON is a sports writer for the *Toronto Star*. She has also done time on *As It Happens* for CBC Radio and contributed the odd piece to *National Lampoon*. Her book, *Foul Balls*, is available at better book stores even as we speak.

ALLAN GOULD was born in 1944 and raised in Detroit. He was driven half-mad with cries of "if you're that good, why aren't you in Canada?" So he moved to Toronto, in 1968, where he has three books to his credit, even though his bank will not advance any, all of them rather funny, his mother thinks.

SERGE GRENIER was born in Montreal, and, chances are, will die there. He became a humourist while studying philosophy at the Université de Montréal, after discovering that Woody Allen was funnier than Plato. After five long years in Ontario, he returned to Quebec, and is now a full-time writer and humourist.

RAY GUY is a writer and broadcaster who lives in St. John's, Newfoundland. A keen observer of Toronto life (through the magic of the national media), he is at a loss to explain it, despite having spent three years at Ryerson.

ED HAILWOOD believes that when you die, your soul goes bowling at Eglinton and Brimley. He is loosely associated with *Toronto Life Magazine*, which has convinced him that the downtown core isn't so hot either.

MATTHEW HART is a living example of the Toronto Work Ethic . . . having left his indelible imprint on *The Globe and Mail*, the CBC (radio and television), the *Ottawa Citizen* and the *Montreal Star*. He is currently at work on a book about Halley's Comet. He loves to talk about cows.

KAYE and RON HEARNDEN were both born in Toronto, where they live with their daughter, Lisa, in a west end 1950s house. Kaye, when not working in retail, is a gourmet cook, while Ron makes and drinks wine.

MICHAEL HOWELL, the immediate past Director of Publicity and Public Relations for the Toronto-based Canadian Opera Company, contributed a few unattributed remarks on life in his adopted city by the shores of Lake Ontario. Born in Texas, he has just completed 13 years in exile in Canada and is returning to the States to contend with another challenging city, New York.

MARNI JACKSON has lived not so much "in" as "under" Toronto for most of her adult life. She is the oldest semi-successful freelance writer extant, although she "still looks twelve." She is co-author of the Clichette cabaret shows *Half Human, Half Heartache,* and the upcoming *Return to Gender.*

JON KALINA, Montreal freelance writer and broadcaster, knows Toronto like the small of his back. He knows its snow-capped mountains, its forests, its huddled masses yearning to be rich.

TERRI MONAHAN is a hack writer, a would-be-dancer, a model, and a martial artist whose only claim to fame is being a native of Montreal.

LES NIRENBERG is, at the moment, living the best way he can in Toronto. He is a frequent producer of funny stories for CBC's *The Journal,* does interviews for the *Subway Review* on CBC Radio's *Variety Tonight*, acts in commercials and runs a thriving industrial video business. He claims it is not an easy thing to be a "Renaissance Man."

IAN PEARSON has lived in Toronto for twelve years since he fled from Edmonton. A former associate editor of *Maclean's,* he now freelances for several Canadian magazines. In his spare time, Ian favours fly fishing, distance swimming, Guiness Stout and pretentious biographical thumbnail sketches.

GRAHAM PILSWORTH a bona fide Torontonian, was able from birth to pronounce the name of the city properly — Trawna. However, real success, the birthright of every Torontonian, has been a titanic struggle for two very Toronto reasons. He has failed to perfect the proper Toronto attitude (smug but apologetic) and he has a talent to amuse in a city that is never amused.

VALERIE ROSEDALE is an apostle of *Creeds,* a founding rock of the Granite Club and a member of the Canadian Distaff Establishment. She has relations in Toronto to whom she will never speak (i.e., Don Harron).

PAUL RUSH has worked in almost all fields of journalism. He's the publisher and editor of the *Financial Post Magazine.* Unable to afford a house in Lawrence Park, he lives in an old house in the Olde Kingsway. His most outstanding achievement in life is a prize for general proficiency in Blessed Sacrement Separate School in 1948.

BRIAN SHEIN is a former editor for *National Lampoon* and author of *The Canadian Book of the Dead* to be published later this year.

DAVID SHERMAN is a journalist who recently spent six months with the CBC in Toronto. Tired of dividing his paycheque between Air Canada, Bell Canada and Revenue Canada, he promised his son he'd never run away from home again and was allowed to return to Montreal.

TINA SREBOTNJAK is an eager and deserving producer with CBC's *Morningside.* She spent her formative years in Mississauga, but has made up for this by travelling extensively throughout the country. Having paid her dues, she now lives in unspeakable contentment in Toronto.

CARSTEN STROUD comes from one of the most récherché districts of Ottawa: Hull. Winner of a National Magazine Award in 1983, he is a frequent contributor to *Quest, Toronto Life, Saturday Night* and other tone publications. Like most Torontonians he loves New York and wishes he could live there.

Thanks to:

Barbara and Daniel who were neglected

Josh and Jon who showed the way

Ann Johnston, who gave advice and counsel

Pamela Chichinskas, Lynette Stokes, J.W.Stewart,
Fawn Duchaine, Sherri Clarkson, Evelyne Hertel,
Kathleen Kryklywy and Sharon Thompson.
They are Eden Press and they made this book work:
cajoling, pleading, threatening and supporting,
sometimes all at the same time

The Authors who made this book a joy to edit

Table of Contents

Paul Grilley, Ronald Reagan's son-in-law,
once said Toronto reminded him of his home town
— Columbia Falls, Montana.

Introduction

Poor Toronto. A nation bristles at the very mention of your name.

You're the banks, the insurance companies, and the dreaded CBC. You're head office, the media conspiracy and the reason oil rigs left Alberta. You're Upper Canada, Hogtown and Buffalo North.

But the worst of your sins is this: Americans like you. They think your clean streets, well-dressed muggers and cozy tree-lined avenues are just swell. You've been called "the most attractive American city." Are you not ashamed?

Many of those who know you well have long memories — very long memories. They knew you when you were just another ugly colonial backwater; when your buildings were short, squat and brick. When your sidewalks rolled up at night. When Sundays were enforced with stale cheese sandwiches.

These people are not buying a Toronto with gold-and-glass skyscrapers, speakeasies and restaurants with thirty-seven kinds of pasta.

Then again, many Torontonians aren't comfortable with the New Toronto either. They drive a Mercedes but worry about not having enough change for the parking meter. Fur coats are too conspicuous so they line their trenchcoats with mink and whine that arthritis made them do it. They've learned to pronounce Pouilly-Fuissé, but in their heart of hearts, they're longing for a nice, cold glass of milk.

— 1 —

Never mind, Toronto. The people who wrote this book recognize an anxious and insecure city when they see one. And they're here to help.

Plumbing the depths of your inadequacies, they've found the reasons for your lack of spontaneity, your wimpy politicians and the Maple Leafs. They can help you with some of your deepest, darkest secrets: bad sex, greedy CEOs and a severe case of New York envy. We've even uncovered your funny bone (buried and somewhat numb), under decades of Wally Crouter jokes.

The time has come to lie back on the couch and relax. Loosen that tailored blouse, that plaid jacket, and enjoy this book.

We're here to say that it's OK to be status-conscious, success-oriented, and just a tad nervous about your neighbours.

You, Toronto, have the mind-set of the future: cautious and concerned, with a beady eye for the bottom line. Or, as Terry Mosher once put it, "It's the only city I know where people leap out of bed and yell 'Thank God it's Monday!' "

Wayne Grigsby

THE GOOD, THE BAD & THE TRENDY

The Toronto Work Ethic

Matthew Hart

In Toronto, it is imperative that you work. If you do not, your hands will be taken away and issued to someone else. That is the word they will use: *issue*. In Toronto, no one would be so crass as to come up to you and say:

" 'Ere you. We're 'ackin your 'ands off. Let's 'ave 'em."

That is what they would be thinking, but they would never phrase it that way. In Toronto, a Hands Reclamation Officer will come up to where you are dozing in your hammock (as if you were in bloody Vancouver), and prod you gently with the tip of his cutlass. And he will say:

"Beggin' your pardon, Sir, but we'll be needin' them 'ands. They're bein' re-issued to them as needs 'em."

And at that point, my lad, you can forget scrambling for the lawn mower, or making those silly swishing gestures with your hands. They will have seen such painful displays before and you will only be embarrassing everyone. This is the Toronto Work Ethic actually working. It is a stern code but, by God, it keeps the snoring down.

Toronto was not always this way. Back in the 18th century, when the French ran the place, it was a veritable cesspool of lassitude.

Voluptuaries poured into the city from Paris and Shanghai and, yes, from Buffalo, crowding into the scandalous dormitories that sagged in silence along the waterfront. Nor was there any moral leadership to be had from the colonial administration.

The infamous Governor, AuLit, himself a measureless pit of somnolence, went so far as to strike a coat of arms bearing a pair of lolling unicorns and the legend *Dormir, c'est moi.*

Happily, the French garrison fell, probably asleep. One morning the squalid nappers awoke to call for their sleeping pills, and found themselves staring up a yard of good English steel with a nasty little hole at the hither end. This is where the phrase "rude awakening" comes from. The simple soldierly desire to get everyone up and on the *qui vive* was mistaken for discourtesy. Many of Toronto's problems originate this way, but never mind. We are not here to slop around in a lot of foppish introspection.

In its early days as a British settlement, Toronto really had no ethic at all. There was a certain amount of energetic drunkenness on the one hand, and on the other the usual gang of sullen oligarchs stirred their toes amidst the bones of the peasantry. Nothing there to *call* an ethic. If there was any dominant principle, it was rapacity. Toronto was to languish this way until the founding of the Toronto Transit Commission. It was the TTC that brought the Work Ethic to Toronto, and it is the TTC that maintains it today.

A lot of people, even native Torontonians, think that the TTC was founded to move people around Toronto. This is not so. It is true that the TTC *will* take you here or there, but only because the drivers are going that way anyway. Otherwise you could find your own way, mate, instead of hanging about subway stations for a lift as if you were the bleeding Prince of Wales.

No, the TTC was founded so that Toronto would have a, well, working model of the Work Ethic at hand. It was an attempt to light a fire under the Catholics.

The problem as perceived by the Family Compact (not a car) was that the Catholics spent altogether too much time swanking around in crimson and hankering after Rome. This, marriage, and making wine pretty well added up to 18 holes on the golf course of Catholic activity. Meanwhile, there were the Eatons, wandering disconsolately around their empty store, where only the crimson cloth department had enough traffic to keep the dust from settling.

It had to stop.
It had to start.

A crack unit of Toronto personnel officers was crowbarred into boiled shirts and packed off to Ulster. In Northern Ireland, in those days, they knew what to do with Catholics. They would build a shipyard and stick 'em inside. There — or so reasoned the leading Belfast thinkers — the sight of so many labouring Protestants would send each Catholic male diving for his own spanner. Recruited in their hundreds, these Ulster Protestants were the famous "Orangemen," so named for their astonishing appetite for citrus and the striking pigmentary anomalies which sometimes ensued.

Right.

The TTC was waiting for them when they arrived, and each man was simply given his streetcar, his bus, his trolley or train, and told to get on with it. This they did, and do still.

In appearance the Toronto Work Ethic is a sort of darkish principle, fabricated from steel girders with plenty of rivets. The Bloor-Danforth viaduct is a good example. It is sturdy and it is straightforward. It stays where it was put, patiently carrying traffic back and forth across the Don Valley, never getting ideas. And over this splendid structure, hundreds of times a day, travels the TTC, bearing the Ethic into the farthest corners of the municipality, where stout, busy-handed dealers wait for it in front of their shops.

In fact, even the Queen has commented on the remarkable hardihood of the Ethic in Toronto. The Royal cavalcade was cannoning through the city on its way to a fun dinner of beef somewhere, when it swept past a TTC crew toiling on the St. Clair line. Here is what happened:

Nothing! Not one pick missed a beat!

Her Majesty's now famous aside, "What are those guys, robots?" is so cherished by the men, that they have had it wood-burned onto one of those wavy-edged signs which now hangs over the entrance to the maintenance shed up at the Davisville yards. For some strange and possibly twisted reason, the Work Ethic and the Royal Visit tend to thrive in the same air, except in Agincourt, where nothing thrives but CFTO-TV and an angry, bitter little strain of grass unknown below Highway 401.

That's it, then. The Work Ethic is here, and anyone who wishes to inspect it may. Just take a Queen car to the corner of Roncesvalles, get out and watch. There you will find the greatest concentration of streetcar tracks anywhere, next to Berlin's legendary Whirligigplatz. Just ask for directions; anyone will help. Unless, of course, he's working.

Call Me Conrad
How To Be Somebody on Bay Street

Ian Brown

Bay Street is the capital of Rosedale and the city's central fixation. If money is the blood of Toronto, Bay Street is its aorta.

The successful Torontonian, boiling over as he invariably is with ambition, understands this fact instinctively. He quickly learns to survive on Bay Street by imitating one or another of Canada's late, but still prominent capitalists, many of whom are buried upright behind their desks. With time, effort, and an inheritance, making it on Bay Street is even easier than it seems.

VOICE   Cultivate one. Speak through the nose, from deep within the forehead. The desired effect — sometimes known as "limousine lockjaw" — can be obtained by inserting two jumbo straws up the nasal passages and reciting writs. While the lips may move, the teeth should remain firmly clenched throughout all conversation, be it professional, romantic, professional/romantic, or romantic/professional.

VOCABULARY   Never use one word where five will do. Don't say "We're in hock up to our knackers," say "I think you'll find our latest issue of convertible preferreds *very* attractive, Bill."

Similarly, "We're restructuring our debt load" is preferable to "What can I say? We've gone tits up."

Eschew profanities like "asshole" except in dire circumstances, as when your next door neighbour, the Attorney General, launches a takeover bid for your family's chartered bank and/or your wife. Use phrases such as "psychiatric Falstaff" and "pitiful prepubescent" instead. "Idiot" or "fool" will do in a pinch.

DRESS If you so desire, but only at late-night meetings of the Law Society of Ontario at the Albany Club. (The question of dresses for women is moot: women do not exist on Bay Street.) Otherwise, the prescribed Bay Street uniform is a white shirt, black shoes (to be worn on the feet only), navy blue three-piece suit, navy blue pin-striped one-piece tie, and underwear with your name tag still sewn into the elastic from boarding school. Suits should be hand-tailored, but baggy and ill-fitting, especially in the crotch.

SEX Bay Streeters do not engage in sex, except as adolescents at selected private boys' schools.

MARRIAGE The old Bay Street rule of thumb — marry once, and never again — is changing with the times. Mutes, however, are still considered to make the best wives, particularly if "horsey."

Wives' names should begin with the letter "B" or "P" — Bunny, Binky, Pussy, Penny and Prue are preferred. They should possess fine pedigrees, independent means, and large hungadungas.

INFIDELITY Infidelity has an honoured but troublesome place within the Bay Street mythos. An executive who successfully engineers a takeover of another corporation automatically gains unlimited access to the wife and daughters of the vanquished CEO, as was the practice with the ancient Aztecs. Taking one's secretary as one's second wife (with or without divorcing the first) is acceptable for those in the legal profession. Nevertheless, public display of one's infidelities, however numerous, is considered tasteless. As always, let hypocrisy be your guide.

RELATIVES Brothers, if unavoidable, should be named Montegu and be of eccentric intelligence. Sisters should be neither seen nor heard, and are best stored in a cupboard at an exclusive "finishing school" in a neutral European country. Fathers may or may not be alcoholic suicides; they must, however, leave you a fortune of not less than $40 million. For one thing, it's virtually impossible not to make at least some money with $40 million in your pocket; with less than $40 million, you stand very little chance of being eternalized in overwritten, overpriced, pseudo-sociological tomes penned by sycophantic arriviste journalists who have changed their names.

DRUGS   Chivas Regal, Valium and vastly aromatic Havana cigars. Marijuana is frowned upon on Bay Street as both adolescent and unpronounceable. Cocaine is for television industry executives who aren't real people.

POLITICS   Depends which party you wish to own. The smart money, however, goes both ways. Never admit to knowing John Turner. On Bay Street, anyone who votes for the NDP is considered a bestialist.

AUTOMOBILES   Small, navy blue Chryslers with dog hairs all over the seats are the preferred auto of the truly wealthy: ostentation is frowned upon on Bay Street. If you *must* drive a Cadillac, install an eccentric ornament in the middle of your Fleetwood's hood — a small, discreet silver sheep from Birks, for instance. When asked what it signifies, reply cryptically: "It's for the wife." This will elicit many "chuckles," the Bay Street equivalent of laughter, from your friends, and will earn you a reputation as a "wit." Rented limos with a spare Negro driver strapped to the roof rack are considered passé. The word *Negro* is not considered passé.

CLUBS   Never, never, never take your golf clubs to work.

DINNER CLUBS   The drearier the better. Inedible food is a must. "Squash" clubs are for vegetables. A club that admits Jews, wogs or Catholics is probably the Ontario Legislature. Shoes must not be (however discreetly) removed for toe-itching during takeover negotiations at one's club. Passing wind to the tune of "O Canada" in two-part harmony in a club's billiard room after a hearty meal of sweetbreads and Jello is perfectly acceptable.

EDUCATION   Private boys' schools only. Upper Canada College and the Palm Springs Outward Bound College are preferred, and the sooner the better. True Bay Streeters leave home for boarding school, equipped with blazers and matching Oedipal complexes, no later than the age of four. By then they should be well up the waiting list for the Toronto Cricket Club.

PREFERRED PROFESSIONS   Law, stocks and the transportation industries. Real estate and the entertainment industries (especially television in its pay and cable incarnations) are frowned upon by Bay Street, as are fast-food executives and high-tech entrepreneurs. Banking is for rubes, consulting is for girls.

   Professions for children should be assigned before the age of six. Females should be routed into charitable work or dressage: males must follow in their fathers' footsteps unless they are homosexual, in which case they must be shot, staked through the heart and buried in oaken boxes, or encouraged to run for public office.

NOMENCLATURE   Bay Street's preferred first name for Chief Executive Officers is Gordon, convertible after the age of forty to Swotty. Nicknames earned at boarding school are considered appropriate appellations for one's CEO during corporate board meetings, unless his nickname was ''Lunchtruck'' or ''Peckerhead.''Calling associates by their initials is frowned upon as overly American. When in doubt, refer to a colleague by his last name or as ''You, sir,'' as in ''You, sir, remind me of our Labrador retriever.''

SALARIES   References to one's salary, or ''K power,'' are considered *declassé* except in specific circumstances, in which case strict auditor-approved formulae must be employed. When reporting income to your golf buddies, multiply salary by two and add thirty percent; when reporting to Revenue Canada, divide by three and subtract the lesser of twenty percent or the value of your great-grandfather's rock collection; when wooing a mistress, multiply by six; when pleading to the wife, divide by four; when applying for a new job, add eighty percent; when talking to Peter Newman, add five hundred percent.

BRODERICK CRANSTON III BARRISTER

POOR CRANSTON SHOULD BE A HAPPY MAN. AS A GRADUATE OF OSGOODE HALL AND HARVARD, HE IS A CORPORATE LAWYER WHO PULLS DOWN A COOL $250,000 AND CHANGE ANNUALLY WHICH ALLOWS HIM TO WRITE OFF LIMOUSINES, CLUB-MEDS, SEASON TICKETS, THE RACKET CLUB AND, GET THIS, HIS 14 A.Y. JACKSON'S PLUS HIS EX-WIFE... AS OFFICE FURNITURE! AND YET, OUTSIDE OF TORONTO'S 'COMMERCE COURT', NOBODY REALLY KNOWS WHO THE HELL CRANSTON IS. AND THE MAN DESPERATELY WANTS TO BE A STAR!

OF COURSE POLITICS ARE OUT. THAT WOULD ENTICE 'THE TORONTO SUN' INTO INVESTIGATING HIS VARIOUS PHILANTHROPIC ACTIVITIES.

SO CRANSTON TRIED BRANCHING OUT AS AN AGENT FOR ATHLETES. AND THEN WHAT HAPPENED? THERE HE WAS, HAVING LUNCH WITH TIGER WILLIAMS IN 'WINSTON'S', TWO TABLES AWAY FROM JOHN TURNER FOR GOD'S SAKE ...AND TIGER BARFED ALL OVER HIS SNAILS!

REQUIRED READING   Histories of monopoly capitalism and fifteen pound studies of the role of horses in war. Avoid success handbooks, guides to making it on Bay Street and the clichéd literature of success like the plague. Where reading is concerned, as with all questions of Bay Street behaviour, one cardinal rule applies: if you have to ask, you don't belong here.

Keeping Up
With the Trendies

Tina Srebotnjak

Everyone wants to be a Toronto trendy — it's one of the ultimate rewards of co-operative federalism. But it's not something you can just leap into. Riding the trends, like playing the horses, can be pretty tricky unless you know how to read the track.

Trendies by definition eschew the pedestrian. They don't have homes; they have "living space." They don't care about the Genies or the Grammies; they follow the design awards. They live for hi-tech. They like grey, white, pink neon (when tastefully appointed), and just to show they've been to Queen Street, black vinyl.

Toronto trendies excel at the fine art of discrimination. They know instinctively when to turn their backs on Gloria Vanderbilt and embrace Calvin Klein. They moved as one away from Haagen-Dazs ice cream and welcomed the newcomer Früdje Glädje. Yes, in an unguarded moment, they did embrace the Punk look, but smartly guided it to the safety of raw silk with just a soupçon of new wave.

This is not to say that trendies are totally fickle, of course. Some things are worth keeping, and, in the face of all pretenders, trendies have stuck by their Gucci Loafers, Sperry Topsiders and Cartier tank watches.

So how do you know when you're in the presence of a true Toronto trendy? Well, the first clue is that they find themselves, and sometimes even each other, utterly fascinating. They love to talk about their Lives (they all live in Upper Case). So plant yourself discreetly somewhere in deepest Yorkville and you're bound to overhear everything essential to this higher form of existence.

You will be struck immediately by the trendies' obsession with their bodies. Sweat, O Canada, is In. Not YMCA sweat, mind you, but the more elegant kind that flows into colour-coordinated designer workout gear. Stripes are very big, as are cute little plastic pants. It's one of the givens of trendy workouts, of course, that you have a great body to begin with. No size sixteen leotards, please.

Headbands should be of the two-toned braided variety, shoes over-priced and thick enough to choke a Saint Bernard. The whole kit and kaboodle should be carried in a discreet maroon SportSac, not the chintzy nylon bag they sent you when you renewed your subscription to *Maclean's*.

Once finished with their workouts, Toronto trendies don their leather pants and slither gracefully toward one of the chic little Toronto eateries for a bite. Caesar salads are very In, as are melon and prosciutto. Spritzers are old hat; they order Kir. Everything in toy quantities, of course. We don't want to get tummies, do we?

Toronto trendies have a battery of personal consultants. Thus, they often start their sentences with "My nutritionist says, . . . My hair analyst says, . . . My vitamin therapist says, . . . " How the sentence ends is neither here nor there, for in grammar, as in life, a smart beginning is everything.

While talking, trendies affect an animated pose, sometimes even using their hands to underline a clever remark. While listening, trendies either suck in their cheeks — and most have cheekbones you could shave with — or they pout. They love restaurants with mirrors.

Toronto trendies get their colours done. Once they discover what "season" they are, they're given a little wallet with all the colours they've been born to wear, and they head straight to Holt's, destined never to make a fashion *faux pas* again. They press their little swatches of colour against Alfred Sung designs to ensure that the garment is truly *them*.

(A word to the wise; trendies may have big bucks, but they're still Torontonians, and in this town, a dollar is still resolutely a dollar. It is *not* trendy to be taken.)

Gourmet eating is big time stuff in Toronto, and as befits a city not world-renowned for its spontaneity, it is a studied affair. On Saturday, trendies all over the city (many of them still in their floor-length terry robes) rush to retrieve the "City Living" section from the *Globe and Mail* to see what spot Joanne Kates has annointed this week. They don't mind going to Chinatown or North Toronto, as long as they can go secure in the knowledge that they're doing the done thing. Nothing, however, not even northern Italian restaurants with names ending in "O" will drag them to Willowdale or Mississauga.

Trendies like treatments. Women go to Mira Linder's Spa in the City for facials, seaweed treatments, aquatherapy and pedicures. The really committed have their feet dipped in warm wax and enveloped in electric slippers for the last word in pampering. Men opt for a soothing massage after a killing game of squash. This kind of stuff keeps trendies in shape for the rigours of the real world and the viciousness of the cocktail circuit.

Not surprisingly, trendies have trendy children — perfect little prodigies dressed in miniscule designer jeans and penny loafers. These children acquire a taste for smoked salmon before they hit kindergarten. By the time they're twelve, they can feign indifference with the best of 'em.

But *feigning* is the operative word here — and would-be trendies take note — for although they like to appear outrageous, deep down, trendies are just good Toronto burghers. They may deliberately leave their grey Mercedes in No Parking zones, but they always pay their tickets. They may bop down to New York once or twice a year for the latest in survival gear, but God forbid they should ever have to use it. There's just no getting around the fact that Toronto lies in the heart of good old wholesome Ontario, where the censor board still reigns supreme, and where laws are not made to be broken.

Got the concept? Good. Now suck in those cheeks.

*T*he Official Toronto Workout is designed to teach you the maximum amount of Attitude in the minimum amount of time. It's stern, ambitious and absolutely will not fail — just like you.

You must wear these clothes, you must never be comfortable and you must push yourself unmercifully.

Do not ad-lib or tamper in any way with these exercises. Spontaneity will be punished.

The Right Look

Sexy but stand-offish. Fitness is implicit here. A cocked hip suggests dancercise, but with none of the sweat. The oversized bag implies a full change of Simon Chang, the leg warmers imply shin splints at some time in her life. This is a look that will reduce snotty boutique owners to whimpering puddles.

The Wrong Look

Note the matted hair, the sodden t-shirt, the bared toes (with unsightly bumps and calluses) and the fully extended leg. This person has perspired. Besides, she looks wimpy. She is also making non-threatening eye contact with us. This *must* be avoided at all costs.

See the difference? Good!

Now it's time to try the Official Toronto Workout.

Exercise
#1

An exercise to maximize that morning kiss 'n ride. In fact, why waste those morning kisses on hubby when you can just as easily do this at home? Sit on the floor, knees open, then lean, pucker and thrust (two more) . . . lean, pucker and thrust (one more) . . . and don't forget to wave.

Exercise
#2

Having trouble with that contemptuous glance? Then learn to look truly aloof with our cheekbone sharpening exercise. Stand with shoulders back in front of a mirror, suck in those cheeks, and blow, (hold, one, two, three) and blow. Suck . . . and blow . . . and suck (keep sneering) . . . and blow. (Please note: if desired effect is not achieved please call 555-3066 for plastic surgery.)

Exercise

#3

Having trouble with your shopping stamina? Tired of looking like the missing link? Get those knuckles off the ground by practising our "Shopping spree" exercise. (Purchase designer barbells directly from us.) Each barbell is balanced to weigh exactly the same as $1,000 worth of Alfred Sung's Pret à Porter. Then grab those bells and S-T-R-E-T-C-H.

Exercise

#4

Own a dog? Tired of Fido's public pecadillos? Turn embarrassment into health with this simple, stylish exercise. Smile. Glance around. Stoop and scoop. (Keep smiling — they're watching.) And scoop. If you don't own a dog, do this anyway, it will improve your bowling game and, if need be, you can check your friends for hernias. (Keep smiling now.)

Exercise

#5

Ambition is just as important in your daily exercise routine as it is in real life. When that golden opportunity presents itself you need to be fighting fit and raring to go. Learn to stomp your way up the Bay Street corporate ladder. Set your sights on your career goal and pick those feet up and up and up (don't look down) and up and up . . .

Exercise

#6

Is your career not going where it should? No problem. We'll show you how to set it right with this simple glozing exercise. Lie on your back, think of who could do you the most good, and roll over. After all, if you can kiss your own, you can certainly kiss someone else's . . . (150 more) . . . roll (149 more) . . . roll . . .

Exercise

#7

We call this the pre-nuptial pelvic exercise. Kneel, centre on the blasé, light up a cigarette and thumb languidly through your most recent issue of BRIDES. Lean way back (feel those tummy muscles pull), and straighten; pull and straighten. (Please note that this is not recommended as a post-nuptial exercise. Why bother after the wedding?)

Exercise

#8

You're now ready to take on the outside world, but remember, you never know who you are going to meet. So, complete your program with the John Turner greeting exercise. He may well be a graduate of the Ottawa School for the Incredibly Good Looking, but he has his little ways. If you do come across him, keep your eyes firmly fixed on his hands (never turn around), draw up one leg, flex your arms, then kick, shouting ''Hyeeeeeee.'' Now you're ready for absolutely anyone.

Photographer: Jennifer Goddard

Diary of a
Nouveau Toronto Housewife

(Gucci, Gucci, Goo)

Marni Jackson

June 15th

Dear Diary:

It's hard to believe, but as of yesterday, I, Trudi Barrington, owner of the Ma Poisson *fish-snack boutique* in the Hazelnut Caves, became a merchant and a mother! We had to close the shop for the day and a shipment of fresh eel went bad, but it was worth it — she's gorgeous. A girl, Veronica Sam (Ronnie for short), nine and a half pounds. Everything went very smoothly and Terry was incredible — breathing with me, jumping rope with me, piling dictionaries on the small of my back to ease the pain (oops, I mean the "sensations") . . . and then just when I felt I couldn't go on, he wheeled in a trolley of Dim Sum. What a sweetie!

We stayed at home as long as possible, wearing our fencing masks and "lunging through" the contractions the way they show you in prenatal class. Around midnight Terry made up a thermos of Kelp tea and some baggies of tabouleh for the hospital, and we phoned Natalie the midwife. She came right over and rubbed me down with sea salt and

Haagen-Dazs chocolate chip ice cream — it really helped. By 3:00 a.m. I was screaming into the duvet so Terry suggested we head out. I changed into my labour outfit (French blue crushed-cotton t-shirt with leg warmers), and Terry packed up the Volvo with all the little birth accessories they tell you to bring to the hospital — popsicles, tennis balls, a live canary, the Betamax, warm sox, a doorstop, small photocopier, etc. I fixed Terry a bacon sandwich, which really made me nauseous, and then we raced off to the TGH.

The Birthing Room nurses were all terrific. They did the Blanket Toss, where they throw you up in the air three or four times, and one of them knew all the words to Grease *and kept singing them at me when I got out of hand — what a panic!*

Ironically, Terry almost missed the big moment — he was taping some set-up shots of the wall-hanging, equipment, etc., when Veronica decided to be born (with me in what they call the "goalie position"). Right afterward we did eye contact, I-Thou visualization, crooning and bonding, then I changed into a simple white chenille robe with ivory ballet slippers, and we phoned everyone. The girls at the shop were thrilled, of course, and they said the new carp quenelles had completely sold out; that made my day complete.

July 2nd

Dear Diary:
Too tired to write much. The baby is cute but not very self-sufficient, . . . always needs to be fed, changed, etc. Hope this is just a phase. Tried getting back into my Alfred Sungs today — not a chance. Threw myself on the bed and told Terry to take the baby to the Dominion; cold air coming off

the frozen-food section seems to calm her down. Terry's getting on my nerves. He burnt the béchamel and put the baby in the Snuggli backwards, getting zipper marks on her chin.

I tried taking Ronnie to the shop, but it didn't work out. Put her down for just a second and a customer tried to buy her! He thought she was a sea-bass. She does look amphibious, but the doctor says all newborns do.

Then I went next door for a capuccino and they said "So when's the baby due?" I burst into tears, . . . this body cost me $1,200 in health-club fees and now it's ruined! Terry said he'd buy me an espresso machine for at home. Big deal! Felt so bad I stopped into La Petite Grenouillerie *on the way home and bought red leather diapers for many $$$.*

August 6th

Dear Diary:
Well, I feel I've finally got the hang of motherhood. Of course, hiring a live-in nanny helps — now I have the time to really work on Veronica in all the special ways you can't when you're busy feeding, changing, bathing, etc. Missy has eight children of her own back in Barbados that she hopes to bring up here, so she is a hard worker — she even restrung my squash racket last week! Of course, there's always a little tension between caregivers *. . . Missy thinks six weeks is too young for the Mitey-Mite fitness classes at 21 McGill. I made them go anyway. But I really can't complain — I pay her $1.75 an hour and she does some light housework, like getting the raccoons out of the attic and dry-walling the spare room.*

My days are a little more manageable now. After I pick out Veronica's clothes, I slip back into bed, Terry leaves for work and Missy takes over. Around ten I go into the shop, make up the tekka-maki trays, go through the orders and then drop by the club for their "Body Back Guarantee" postnatal fitness classes. Missy and the baby catch up with me in a cab for some crosstown breastfeeding, then I may lunch with a wholesaler, or just browse through the shops and pick up dinner at Noblesse Oblige *on the way home. At 6:30 I have a nice 40-minute play with Veronica, making her track objects with her eyes, point to different parts of her body, and grasp simple toys. Then Missy pops her into bed and Terry and I enjoy a real dinner à* deux, *the way we used to. (Missy has a card table in the den and will only eat* Lean Cuisine *so that's no problem. She didn't like the futon I bought for her, however — "Oh, Mrs. Barrington, I would like some legs for my bed," she said. One forgets the culture gap!)*

September 14th

Dear Diary:
Birthday party at the Huckster's for their little boy Darvey. Veronica and Darvey had a nice little session of Parallel Play while the parents ate a wonderful Cajun brunch and discussed squeeze-toys. Darvey's gross motor skills are quite impressive; wish we'd worked harder on Veronica's. Her rooting is strong but her flexing could be better.

Jackie and I did some texture-play with them, cutting up her old silk blouses for them to experience. The Hucksters love their new au pair; *she's an Early Childhood Education grad who really knows how to stimulate. I think if you just treat babies as* little people *they never have to go through that childish phase.*

I was telling Jackie how out-of-control my grooming has been since the baby, and she suggested I book into L'Heure

Précieuse *spa for a day's overhaul. Apparently they have a special "Toddler-Coddler" program for babies — brow tints, a rash workshop and a back-to-the-womb room where they float them in brine and play heartbeat tapes. Meanwhile, I'm lying next door having a herbal wrap and a bikini wax. Sounds fabulous.*

October 24th

Dear Diary:

Ronnie talked today! It just goes to show that letting them sleep with the Walkman on really speeds up their verbal development. Her first sentence was "nigh-nigh 'nart" ("night-night, Cuisinart"). She always has to say goodnight to the appliances before she goes to bed.

November 20th

Dear Diary:

Took Ronnie to see Daddy's office on Bay Street. She was so excited! "Hur' my eyes," she kept saying as we drove down towards the Royal Bank building with the sun on all that glass. She said Terry's office tower looked like a "big, big, big toilet," and she called his desk "Daddy's crib." She had a great time playing in the broadloom. Then the three of us went out for lunch at Neri, *the new black-pasta restaurant. Liked everything but the black bean soup.*

February 4th

Dear Diary:

Brunch at the Levison's yesterday — packed with babies! It seems everyone has one these days. I brought along our new smoked whitefish and Portuguese periwinkles, which were devoured in a flash. Jessica's little boy was wearing those new baby dentures (for late teethers), which I thought was a bit much. Alison brought along the new Fischer-Proust *Activity Centre, which shows your baby how to buy RRSPs and do simple banking — it's really cute. Ronnie showed off a little on her* Pro-Tyke *word processor, and then she asked me if she could sleep over with Darvey. I said only if she cared for him very, very deeply. Being a parent is so tricky!*

March 2nd

Dear Diary:

Well, we had to let Missy go. She got very upset when I spoke to Veronica about infant sex. I know nine months seems young, but kids grow up faster these days — and I didn't really go into details, I simply gave her an excellent new Baby-Board book called Squish! *which uses simple imagery to explain reproduction. Missy threw the book out and kept yelling at me that "babies are babies." Well, of course I know that. I try to give Veronica lots of "baby time" to roll around and play by herself. I give her flour and water paste to dabble in. Missy thinks playing silly games and singing and talking is all there is to it — she has no idea what infants are capable of if you give them a little direction. She refused to use the Nautilus baby-bar-bells I bought, and she claims the Walkman gives Ronnie headaches. When I explained that children are very right-brained in the first place, she gathered up her sewing, went into her room and closed the door. Honestly, you try hard to be the best sort of employer you can be with your help, but they're so set in their ways. Of course, Veronica is upset but we promised to send her to Rhythm Camp this summer, so that cheered her up.*

September 6th

Dear Diary:

The house feels so empty now that Veronica has gone to boarding school. At first I thought I might wait another half-year, but with the new shop opening up in the Eglinton Concourse, things are going to be too hectic at home. I think the challenge will be good for her too. She was getting awfully dependent on us, and even though I let her work the cash at the shop, the girls were losing their patience with her. They have horses at the school; she will enjoy that. We decided against the wire-mesh columns to break up the entrance to the new shop and put in smoked-glass mirrors instead — it works much better. When she left, we told Ronnie "See you at Christmas," and she said "Where's Christmas?" What a cutie!

THE WAY WE WERE

Once upon a time in Toronto, vichyssoise was just cold potato
soup, and no dinner was complete without a pickle tray.
Back then, non-WASPs knew their place and stayed there with
a minimum of grumbling.
We toasted the Queen at dinner and stood for her anthem
before movies.
We drank rye and scotch and worshipped faithfully: the
Gardens on Saturday night; the United Church of our choice on
Sunday morning.
Wayne and Shuster were funny then. And "gay" meant happy.
But that was long ago—when you had to have the right kind of
British accent to live in Rosedale.
That was The Way We Were.

A Souvenir of Lawrence Park

Paul Rush

I remember the day Aunt Alicia saw the Othello.

It was the autumn of 1950, and she told me about it as she sat in the kitchen of Grandma Kormann's big old house, furtively smoking a cigarette. Grandma Kormann, an invalid, lived upstairs and didn't approve of smoking — or much else. Aunt Alicia's role in life was ministering to her needs.

"There he was," said Aunt Alicia, the cigarette held at the very end of her first two fingers, "right at the corner of Yonge and St. Clair. But I didn't stare at him."
"What's an Othello?" I asked.
Aunt Alicia looked at me with concern. Smoking was her only vice. Then she took a breath: "He was . . . black."

In the same vein, my mother, Alicia's sister, would in those years sell the plum tree in our back yard every summer. Rather, she would sell the picking of its fruit. She would, as she put it, ring up "the Chinaman," and he would come over and assess the tree. He and my mother would haggle for a bit, agree on a price, and then he would call his children to do the picking. To my mother he was "the Chinaman" because he was the only Chinese person she actually knew. She was vaguely aware that there might be another "Chinaman" behind the counter in the laundry on Yonge Street, but she never went there because every Wednesday morning "the laundryman," a chap called Mr. Parker, came by the house to pick up a big bundle tied in a sheet.

There were also the ashmen, the garbagemen, the breadman and the milkman. The latter being such a regular on the route that every Christmas Eve he was poured so many drinks he could barely move. Luckily, he knew the way.

In those days, the Toronto after World War Two, everyone had a slot they fitted into. For example, my mother engineered a move to a house in a classier neighbourhood only four blocks from our old house. As a young child, uprooted from my friends, I asked her why. And I remember her answer: "Well, dear, that neighbourhood wasn't quite right for us, what with your father being a King's Counsel. There was a policeman living just around the corner and Mr.— across the street did something in a factory."

Toronto society, as interpreted by my mother, had rigid boundaries and strict codes. It was proper and fitting to be a lawyer and it was best to be a judge. Being a doctor or dentist was also acceptable, although better the former than the latter. It was acceptable to be a university professor, borderline to be a high school teacher, and infra dig to teach in primary school. (Unless, of course, you were a nun.)

The important thing was to have a profession. Thus one could be an accountant, a bank manager, or even a teller (they had expectations). But the civil service, trade, selling, or running a shop were below the social salt.

For example, my mother dealt with one small shopkeeper for perhaps forty years. He was a client of my father's, and he and his wife would often drive my mother to church in her later years. Yet he never made it past "Thank you, Mr. O'Connor, . . ." One didn't encourage familiarity.

As Catholics, always aware of our somewhat precarious social standing, we had a special spot for priests and nuns high up the social ladder. We also had a number of them in the family — aunts, uncles and cousins — and on utterly dead Toronto Sundays we would go to visit them. Aunt Geraldine, lively and vivacious, lived in St. Joseph's convent on Wellesley Street, then with a fence and an orchard, now the site of an Ontario government complex. Aunt Tessie, from the same order, was crippled with arthritis and lived on the Scarborough Bluffs in a vast and echoing building with funeral-parlour furniture and creaking floors. Sister St. Edward, bluff and hearty and large, was someone of importance at St. Michael's Hospital.

On Sundays, early in the year, we looked forward to candies from her Christmas supply. But as the year wore on our eagerness was tempered because the chocolates in the box — "Just one each, children" — began to develop furry little white spots.

In those days, large and hearty nuns were the rule. Tough, too. There was Mother Thomas Aquinas, principal of our school, who was large, hearty, tough and hairy, and ran a school that tiptoed in terror of her backhand with the recess bell. It was a profitable shop. Every spring she sent us trudging out with burlap sacks to collect scrap paper to be sold to finance school projects.

In any recollection of my childhood in Toronto, shopping deserves mention. For example, my mother rarely went shopping when it came down to food — she made a list and then she sat down at the phone and called the grocer and the Chinaman and the butcher. In several hours their trucks rolled up and their men trundled around to the back door. There was a great interest when the first supermarket in our area opened (on Yonge Street, about 1947), but my mother regarded it more as a gallery where you went to get ideas rather than as a place to actually buy. Besides, they didn't deliver.

When my mother spoke of "going shopping" she meant putting on a suit, gloves, and a hat with a veil, and taking the two-ticket bus downtown. These major weekly expeditions included lunch (although she might have called it "luncheon") at the Georgian Room or the Arcadian Court in Eaton's or Simpson's.

I was never included — these trips took place while I was at school. But if my mother was going to be late, Aunt Alicia took over and would be perched in the kitchen on the edge of a chair smoking her furtive cigarette when I got home. Wondering, possibly, if I were old enough to be told of the existence of Othellos.

by David Cobb

Toronto's TOP 40 Clichés

This year	Last year	Ten years ago	Cliché	⊘ Coming on strong
1	1	40	Hating Toronto is the only thing that holds this country together	
②	-	-	To dome or not to dome	
3	2	-	It's high time we made the Metro Chairman accountable to the people	
4	10	19	The City That Works	
5	14	-	As Jane Jacobs says . . .	
⑥	23	-	What the hell do the 'burbs know about the city anyway?	
7	8	6	Torontonians are so *cold!*	
8	6	7	Torontonians never smile	
9	5	8	Torontonians never look you in the eye	
10	17	25	The Bay Street power-brokers	
11	11	11	The subways are so clean	
⑫	30	-	When I move downtown I'm going to get rid of my car and walk everywhere	
13	13	37	Frankly, I get a nosebleed north of Eglinton	
⑭	22	-	Go to the CN Tower? Hell no, we *live* here!	
15	16	-	This year we're really going to try to get to the Ex	
16	29	-	I don't know how people can *stand* Spadina Cantonese any more	
17	21	26	It's a city of neighbourhoods	
18	7	-	Hollywood on the Humber	
19	12	4	Take a ferry to the islands and it's like you're in another world	

20	9	3	The streets are safe at night
21	20	-	Your colourful dancers have certainly enriched the cultural diversity of this city
22	19	5	I like them fine as people but they don't do much for real-estate values
23	18	-	The Bay-Bloor axis
24	24	9	The Rosedale Matron
25	27	10	Scarberia
26	28	-	The Yorkville Set
27	15	2	Toronto the Good
28	25	12	They roll up the sidewalks at ten
29	4	21	This is where federal governments stand or fall
30	31	15	Let's take a breakfast meeting at the Courtyard Café/Sutton Place/Park Plaza
31	3	9	Say this for the Tories: they run a good province
32	39	38	Forty years of the same party is just undemocratic
33	38	-	Looking back on it now, I think Sewell was right
34	-	-	The Carlton Street Cashbox
35	-	-	Arrr - gos!
36	-	-	Montreal's a mistress, Toronto's a wife
37	-	-	In Montreal there are two solitudes; in Toronto three million
38	26	4	The best thing about Toronto is the 3:15 train to Montreal
39	26	1	Hogtown
40	40	39	Athens of the North

BUBBLING UNDER: Why do you people run down your city so much?

Those Were the Days

Allan Gould

To be frank, the Toronto of, let us say, twenty-five years ago, was not interesting at all. Critics used to be rather harsh. "The sidewalks of Toronto are rolled up at 10 p.m.," they'd joke. Not so — it was more like 7:15 p.m. sharp. Yes, the rolling up of the sidewalks occurred early back in the 1950s. In fact, it was the highlight of the day. After dragging themselves to work and then home, Torontonians would stuff themselves with Yorkshire pudding and tea and walk slowly (everything was done slowly a quarter-century ago) to their windows to watch the workmen crank the sidewalks under the roadways, only to crank them out again early the following morning. (Actually, it wasn't so much that the streets were particularly safe in those days; it was just that there was no reason to go out.)

People came from around the world to gawk. Not at the sights — back then there was no CN Tower, no Eaton Centre, no Hazelton Lanes and Yorkville, no major zoo . . . no, people came to gawk because few had seen a city where time had stopped. It is not by chance that such Hollywood films as *Night of the Living Dead*, *One Million BC*, and *The Day the Earth Stood Still* were filmed in this town: design costs were nil.

Take Sundays. (Criminals used to be given a choice: ten years in jail or one year of Sundays in Toronto. You can guess what they chose.) In his recent book, maker of TV and film documentaries Harry Rasky writes about growing up in the Toronto of the '40s and '50s. One Sunday, the young Rasky went into a park, where he climbed onto a swing. A policeman rushed over to him. "Young man," he warned, "in Toronto nobody swings on Sunday." The officer couldn't have been more correct, and Rasky never forgot what he said. In fact, he was so impressed by the declaration that he made it the title of his book: *Nobody Swings on Sunday*.

Even Albert Einstein visited Toronto in the early '50s because he'd heard from so many people that Sundays here lasted thirty-three hours. Einstein was thrilled to discover that his theory of relativity was correct. "A Sunday in Toronto certainly *seems* to last over thirty-three hours," he later wrote in his notebooks.

However, Sunday in Toronto in the '50s was heaven for religious leaders because churches were the only places open (there were ugly rumours that even the churches were closed, but these were crude fabrications). But Toronto Sundays were hell for everyone else. Did the visitor — or even the resident — care to see a movie? They could forget it. Go to the theatre? Not on your life. Have a drink? Perish the thought. Dine out? In a hotel perhaps, but nowhere else. Even most of the greasy spoons were closed.

All people could do on Sunday was to pray. Tourists prayed they'd never be tempted to return here again. Businessmen prayed they'd be sent to Detroit, Buffalo, Pittsburgh — *anywhere* — on their next trip. And citizens of Toronto prayed that the city would join the 20th century some time in the near future.

From the escritoire of

Valerie Rosedale

As an avid gardener, I am always just a teensy bit apprehensive about digging too deep around one's roots. The particular area in which I live (and we are extremely particular), provides a rich soil for the spreading of myth, rumour and innuendo. But begone dull fear, it's time to tell the truth about the most exclusive WASP ghetto in Canada.

(Let me state at the start that I loathe the acronym I have just used. I am not a White Anti-Sexual Protestant; I think of myself as an Anglican-Saxophone.)

The literal bounds of the subdivision of Rosedale, the truly greater part of Greater Metropolitan Toronto, vary according to real estate values. Basically speaking, we start north of Bloor on the south, Yonge Street on the west, the Don Valley Parkway on the east, and we blend almost imperceptibly north of St. Clair Avenue with a mixture of new and old money that waits patiently on our fringes hoping against hope to displace us. During the socially ambiguous sixties, our confines were pierced by barbarians converting our stately mansions into rooming houses, but recent recessions and government restraint programmes seem to have redressed and restored the fiscal imbalance.

Too late for me and mine, alas. Hubby and I fled Rose-hippy-dale as soon as our only issue, Stephanie, fell out of the nest into the boarding school system. After graduating minima cum laude from the Loathsome Hall (I'm a Loathsome Old Girl myself) our Steff was dispatched by us to learn Québecois at Neuchatel in Switzerland. Unfortunately, she fell in with a

Valerie Rosedale

bunch of B.S.S.'s (there seems to be a lot of that around these days) and came home to us last June with no French at all and a rather peculiar rash. So much for cultural exchange.

Loathsome Hall, by the way, has built an unnatural bridge over the Mount Pleasant Expressway, linking the two solitudes of Rosedale, east and west. The construction, which juts out over the roadway high above the traffic, allows the girls to make their pedestrian way to or from school. The structure itself has been dubbed the Bridge of Thighs by passing motorists who crane their necks ever upward at our kilted schoolgirls, who pass intacta far above the madding throng of auto-erotics.

The expressway itself is a means of funnelling the lower and middle classes through our little principality, as they zoom north from the bowels of commerce to their lumpen-bourgeois substandard dwellings. Do I digress? I merely wanted to state that Mount Pleasant was originally a rustic laneway given over to the furtive grapplings of lovers, but the active verb in its title has given way to its reduced role as a mere noun.

Heavens to Queen Betsy, I'm supposed to be giving you the historic origins of Rosedale! To do that, one must go back to the American Bolshevik-type Revolution of 1776, when those who counted remained true-blue Tory in the face of all those Liberal excesses performed by so-called Republican Rebels, who sound more like Democrats to me.

We called ourselves United Empire Loyalists, but the Yankees dubbed us Draft Dodgers. They told us to go to Hell, Hull, or Halifax. Since we were on our Uppers anyway, my family chose that part of Canada which best suited our status, and we settled in the village of Yorkville, which sounded like a lovely place to browse and shop.

Valerie Rosedale

The mayor of this place, however, presented problems. William Lyon Mackenzie was a reckless radical, whose chief pleasure seemed to be driving the Family Compact up the wall. This was not a cheap car but an expensive governing body of bluebloods. I am not surprised to find that he was also the one behind the Rebellion of 1837, and that he later became the natural grandfather of William Lyon Mackenzie King, the shortest Prime Minister of Canada with the longest run in office. Both ran off to the States at the first sign of military action (1837 and 1914) without so much as a green card. Suffice it to say that both returned to this country after the danger was over to resume their gritty political careers.

But such leftish events succeeded in breaking up the old Yorkville crowd, most of whom meandered over to Jarvis Street, or congregated in front of the Horticultural Pavilion in Allen Gardens, where bananas are still raised with regularity, even during the winter months. The tradition of Jarvis Street walking was later institutionalized with the erection of a Night School, Have-a-Gal College, operated by an efficient series of instructresses under the supervision of a Head Mistress. It is sad to note that this venerable body of houses was eventually condemned by the Board of Health and sold to the CBC (which is surely condemnation enough) shortly after the V-J Day excesses of 1945.

By that time the missed carriage trade had settled north of the stews of commerce. As we trekked north with our pots of gold, I would like to report that our grandmummies and daddies found a vale of roses at the end of the rainbow. But there was far more jack-in-the-pulpit, and simply trillions of trilliums, for the illegal plucking.

The few roses that did exist, grew wild, unlike the cultivated ones that abound now. I have managed to keep one wild rose in my compound, my husband Charles, who is an

Valerie Rosedale

absolute terror to snakes when he loses his temper. I don't know how many times he's had his secretary on the carpet, and I can't imagine why, because I'm told by her associates that the girl is really an awfully good head. But I digress again.

Since my surname is Rosedale, the editor of this fluffy tome assumed that I would be privy (ugh!) to all of my sub-division's secrets. Alas, I have a dreadful confession to make. I was born Valerie Rose Farquharson and when I was dubbed a deb I looked for the means of jettisoning my surname. When I met Charles Moultrie Dale at a U.C.C. dance (that's Upper Crust College), we made a mutual proposal of merger before the night was over, and became engaged on the spot. There was no ring forthcoming until Charles joined the Navy and mailed me, not a Birks diamond, but a sweet little pin with two semaphore flags done in blue and white rhinestones. I looked up the message on those flags in "Jane's Fighting Ships," and the engagement was delayed by me for three years because the message read: "Permission to lay alongside and come aboard."

However, the legal merger took place shortly after D-Day (D for Diamond, of course) and we united our surnames into one, with a hyphen between the Rose and the Dale. This was dropped during the honeymoon, as is the custom, when I gave up my hyphen forever.

Although we still keep a "peed a tare" (French for those of you who aren't Bi-) in Rosedale, most of our time is spent a good forty miles north of the city at our estate in King Township in the County of York. There I reign happily as the Queen of the King and ride to hounds as the Stirrup Mistress of York Hunt.

We are content to be away from the excesses of the ef-fluent society, which are soon to be heightened by the addition

Valerie Rosedale

of yet another high-interest-rise bank tower, presided over, as all Canadian banks seem to be, by some lower-middle-class boy from the Maritimes who never got past grade twelve in publicly supported co-educational school (ugh! ugh! ugh!).

But our thoughts often stray to our lovely city enclave which smells all the sweeter partly because of its name, and partly because we made a deal with the city to pick up our garbage at the back door, thus permitting us to put up an uncontaminated front. Here's to you, dear Rosedale! Up you and yours!! As the poet said:

"Surely for you among the saints, will be a special niche,
Who had the courage to espouse the causes of the rich."

V.

Things We Miss...

Kaye & Ron Hearnden

Stock boys on roller skates at the Yonge and Davenport Canadian Tire

Baseball at Maple Leaf Stadium

New car introductions at the CNE

Ritz Carlton Red Hots at the Honey Dew

Sunnyside

Vaudeville shows at Shea's (the big organ rising through the floor)

The Victory (Burlesque's last gasp)

Midnite Holiday Double Header movies

Bobsledding in High Park

Caboose cars on Yonge Street (TTC cars with furnaces on Rogers Road)

Double ender cars on Lansdowne (you could sit at the back and pound away on the foot pedal for the bell)

Brown bagging it at the dances at Mart Kenny's Ranch

Dancing and fighting at the Palace Pier — before it was a condo

Club Top Hat

The Winter Garden (long white gloves)

The "Old" Club Kingsway (remember Wally Koster? Bucky the Bouncer?)

Fallingbrook Dance Hall

Balmy Beach Canoe Club

Ramona Gardens

Strathgowan Badminton Club

The Chicken Palace and "ORIGINAL" Picken Chicken

Moorings

Harry Berberian

Hans Freid and the Sign of the Steer

KIK Cola at five cents

Stone Ginger Beer in stone bottles

Vernors Ginger Ale in cups at Sunnyside

Cincinnati Cream Beer

Canada Bud Ale

Pellers "Ice"

Dawes Black Horse Ale

Jazz at the Plaza Room

Jazz at the Colonial

The King Cole Room (KCR)

Roller skating at Mutual Arena

Chips in a cone at Sunnyside — with salt, a skewer and malt vinegar

Chicken Pot Pie at Arcadian Court

The Round Room at Eaton's College Street

Corned Beef sandwiches at the original Shopsy's on Spadina

All-you-can-eat spaghetti for $1.00 at the Brown Derby

Pilot Tavern

Stoodleigh's Restaurant in the Toronto Star Building

Child's Cafeterias

Scholes Restaurant (Hot Beef sandwiches)

Bowles Lunch

Le Coq d'Or

Bassel's

Roof Dining Room at the Park Plaza

Hall's Dairy (and their trucks which were shaped like milk bottles)

Caulfield's Dairy

Donlands Dairy

Blantyre Dairy

Olive Farm Dairy

City Dairy

Fairglen Dairy

Ford's Dairy

Borden's Dairy (in the Kingsway)

Toronto Telegram (Ted Reeve, Major Hoople, Pink Tely)

Eaton's Main and College Street stores

Frederick's (lingerie and doorman)

Ford Hotel

Walker House

The Casino

THE MOSAIC:
PASTA, PRETZELS
PIEROGIS & PILSNER

Don't worry,
the United Empire Loyalists will rise again.
And when they do,
we'll fix 'em up with a Caravan pavillion.

LA VERA STORIA DI TORONTO

Being the Real History of Toronto
as Told to

Elizabeth Cinello
by her Grandmother

The Founding of Toronto

In 1498 Giovanni Caboto, the Venetian navigator and explorer, set sail with his crew on a voyage that was to shape the lives of all Torontini to come. After a long and arduous trip Caboto disembarked on a flat plain caressed by an untamed lake. His crew, all natives of Taranto, a port city in the Italian region of Puglie, named the site "Yorco" in honour of Sergente Yorco, a well respected sailor and who accompanied Caboto on that historical voyage. Eventually, as the crew settled in the area, they sent for their wives, children, parents, grandparents, uncles, aunts and cousins. Soon almost everyone in this Italian colony had roots in Taranto. By 1834, Italy decided to rename the capital of the colony in honour of all these settlers. Later the name was distorted by various ethnic groups and the town became known as Toronto.

Toronto As A Cittadina

Throughout the 16th century, thanks to the assiduous work of Italian architects, craftsmen and artisans, Toronto flourished as one of the most important trading centres in North America. Plans for Toronto's urban development were based on studies by Leon Battista Alberti, as well as architectural designs by Bramante and Raffaello. While other major North American cities such as New York were considered relatively unhealthy, where houses still had outdoor toilets and garbage was thrown on the streets to rot, Toronto's sewage system enjoyed world-wide acclaim. The Italian Loyalists living in the colony were wise enough to employ the ancient designs of their Roman ancestors for the construction of aqueducts. Toronto's streets were also enriched by elegant architectural masterpieces created by Bernini and Borromini. Unfortunately all the works of these illustrious artists vanished in The Great Fire of 1849.

Toronto And Its Neighbours

By the beginning of the 17th century Alto Canada was populated by Italians, a handful of British in a few insignificant settlements, and Native Indians. For an overall picture of the demographic scale of Canada one must not overlook the French in Basso Canada. Often our Italian founding fathers were involved in arguments with their French neighbours over who produced the best wines. Not infrequently, the French Canadians boasted that they had the finest cuisine on the continent. Their impertinence annoyed Italian Loyalists no end.

Unlike the French settlements, the British settlements posed no problems for our ancestors; the English were usually too drunk to fight. Often, Italian merchants who travelled extensively in Alto Canada would comment about the British. "Give them a bottle of rum, take their money and run."

Early Italian traders got along famously with the Indians in the area. In exchange for being taught new hand signals, Italians taught the Indians some of our traditional dances, such as the Tarantella.

The Simeco' Family

In 1793, Conte Giovanni Simeco' of the Savoia family was sent to the colony. His task was to reinforce the capital of Alto Canada with a fortress. To this end he designed Fort Yorco using a scaled-down version of Michelangelo's plans for Florence. Unfortunately, during its construction, a group of officials from a nearby British settlement cunningly penetrated the fortress and stole the much talked about plans. Simeco' was not terribly concerned as he felt the British would be unable to read and understand the plans, let alone execute them. History confirms his intuition; the plans were never returned and the project never completed.

During their three-year stay the Simeco' family contributed much to the history of Toronto. The first road that Conte Simeco' built was Via Yongo. It was named after Il Marchese Giorgio Yongo, also of the Savoia family. Conte Simeco' named the Humberto river and the Don Corleone river (the Don for short). Signora Simeco' named her home in Toronto Castelfranco as a joke. Today Castelfranco High School stands on the site. She also gave the Scarboro Bluffs their name because they resembled the white cliffs of her home in Scarboro, Calabria. Signora Simeco's diary and her paintings accurately reflect our forefathers' opinions of life in the new capital. She writes:

> If Dante had known of this country he would surely have placed all the sinners of the world in its midst. In the winter a strange substance called "ice" invades the city and its countryside. It freezes all living things in its path. One might liken it to the plague which so devastated Europe. If one survives the ice one must confront the snow which falls from the heavens like the wrath of our Lord upon the transgressors of divine laws. One of the most unbearable aspects of living in the colony is the lack of bidets. Alas! This country is surely for the bears.

Over one hundred years later the eloquent Gabriele D'annunzio visited Toronto, and dedicated one of his most famous lyrics to the city and its countryside. He came, he conquered and he wrote:

Snow in the Maplewood

Hush, On the edge of the wood
I do not hear human words
that you are saying;
but I hear newer words
which far-off flakes and
leaves are speaking.
Listen. It is snowing from
the scattered clouds.
It snows on the smooth birch trees
on the rough, prickly pines,
on the patriotic maples
on the ever upright corn cob
on the odorous berries,
it snows upon our wild faces
it snows upon our naked hands,
on our heavy clothes
on the cold thoughts which the soul, renewed
discloses, on the lovely fable
that yesterday beguiled you, that today
beguiles me, O Toronto, O Canada,
we stand on guard for thee.

Years later, to commemorate the poet's visit to Toronto and to celebrate his masculinity, the C.N. Tower (short for Cosenza-Napoli Tower) was erected in his honour.

The War of 1812

On April 26, 1812, fourteen American ships invaded Toronto. Their goal was to destroy the Italian oceanliner *The Isacco Broccoli*. Unfortunately, the Italian soldiers were not prepared for the attack, as they were at that moment having their uniforms tailored by Michele Armani (great-grandfather of Georgio). However, the invasion was a friendly one, and before a shot could be fired the Americani exchanged their bubble gum, chocolate and nylons for wine. This was truly Toronto's darkest hour.

However, some casualties did occur. The generale Americano Zebulon Pike, looking for a drink, stuck his head in a wine barrel and drowned. The Americani left five days later.

The Rebellion of 1837

In 1820, a Neopolitan named Guilliemo Leone Makenzi began to publish a newspaper called *La Nuova Colonia*, in which he attacked the powerful Family Compact which controlled the government of Alto Canada. Consequently, he was very popular with the poor of Toronto, but despised by the rich (so much so that a group of young men wearing black shirts — the sons of Toronto's wealthy elite — ransacked his newspaper office and destroyed his press). Matters came to a head when, in 1827, Mackenzi spotted Vesco Stracano's (pronounced Strawno) only daughter, Giullietta, at Mario's Groceteria. They fell in love, but unfortunately, Stracano was a member of the Family Compact and an enemy of Mackenzi. Stracano would not hear of his daughter's love for a Neopolitan and contracted a marriage for her with another member of the Family Compact.

This so enraged Mackenzi and his supporters that they pledged to wage war against the Stracano Family, and to this end they organized the Partito Riformista. By 1839, Mackenzi and his Partito had won the Governo Responsabile for Alto and Basso Canada. At last Mackenzi and Giulietta were united. As for Garibaldi, he left for Argentina after Makenzi's wedding to continue the fight for freedom and unity. In recognition of Garibaldi's assistance in the Ribellion del 1837, Makenzio erected a statue of his friend, mounted on his trustworthy horse. Today this statue stands at what is now known as Parco della Regina.

Timoteo Eatone

In 1867, Timoteo Eatone stood on the Southwest corner of Via Yongo and Via Regina and began to preach to his fellow Torontini:
"In the name of the Lord, conquer the heavens by shopping mail order. The Holy Spirit shall descend upon you via Canada Post. Bring a little bit of heaven into your living room. Buy Paradise at Eatone!"
His sermon captured Torontini, and indeed all of Canada, by storm. The following day newspaper headlines read "Canada united by shopping *a mare usque ad marem.*" Shortly after his death, Timoteo was canonized for this accomplishment. Years later, St. Timoteo Eatone church was erected on Via St. Clair in his honour. Even today one can visit his shrine at The Centro Eatone, built in 1977. It is widely believed that pilgrims who kiss the foot of the saint's statue will encounter great fortune in their lifetime, as well as have their line of credit increased by his store.

Toronto's Privileged Citizens

Many important people followed the Simeco' family to Toronto. They include Jack Scaddingo, whose servants' quarters, built in 1794, still stand on the CNE grounds; Guilliemo Osgoodo, first Chief Justice of Alto Canada; Guilliemo Jarvisa, primo secretario dello provincia; Gesse Keciummo who built Toronto's first large factory — Gesse Keciummo's

Ricotta Cheese Factory; la famiglia Massi; Joe Blooro, who opened Toronto's first winery (producing a very popular wine named Spumante Mammina DOC), and Vescovo Giovanni Stracano, Toronto's first Catholic bishop. The bishop built Collegio Triniti, a private boys' school which today is part of the Universita' di Toronto, where two internationally renowned professori, Marcello Macluno and Nortropo Fritto, taught for many years.

Toronto Matures

During the next 150 years, Toronto grew and matured with the times. In 1914, the city built what is popularly referred to as the ROM. Its original name, "Roma Imports," was dropped after the neon sign on the roof lost the letter "a," when a bulb burned out.

In 1931, Cono Smithi acquired the San Patrizio Soccer Team and renamed it the Mapolefi. Nineteen sixty-five marked the construction of the new City Hall, the design of which was based on blueprints by Leonardo Da Vinci. Unfortunately, researchers were able to find only half of his plans — which accounts for the building's semi-circular shape.

Post-War Immigration and Multiculturalism

By the end of the Second World War, 80 percent of Toronto's population was of Italian descent. However, by the beginning of 1970 it had dwindled to just half that figure. Historians attribute this dramatic decline to the waves of immigration in the 1950s and '60s.

Like their Roman forefathers, Torontini were enthusiastic about the idea of a multicultural society, and they consequently opened the doors to immigrants from many European countries such as England, Scotland and Ireland. These new immigrants saw Toronto as a place of opportunity where they could escape the economic depression of their own countries and offer their children a better life in a new land.

Many Irish immigrants moved to the east end of their city, where they grew cabbages on their front lawns. (The Torontini could never understand this preference for cabbages over tomatoes.) The area soon became known as Cabbagetown.

The Scots, who also began to immigrate to Canada in the 19th century, were a major cultural challenge for the Torontini, unaccustomed as they were to the sound of bagpipes and the sight of kilts. (The only

Italians to play bagpipes were shepherds, who used them to entertain their sheep.) Relations between the Scots and the Torontini were often strained; kilted Scottish men were sometimes pinched while taking their Sunday morning strolls.

The Inglesi

The largest ethnic group in Toronto today is the British. At least one out of every ten people in Toronto is of English descent. In the 1950s, British immigrants settled in an area of the city called Rosedale, often referred to by Torontini as "Little England."

In accordance with Toronto's multicultural reality, the Heritage Language Programme was initiated. This programme offered children of British descent the opportunity to study their mother tongue at school. It is only because of the efforts of enlightened Italians that, here and there, English can still be heard in the streets of Toronto.

Under the auspices of this democratic, multicultural policy, the publishing of ethnic language newspapers such as *The Globe and Mail, The Toronto Sun* and *The Toronto Star* flourish as never before. Unfortunately, however, these newspapers enjoy only a limited readership as they cannot compete with the national dailies — *Il Corriere Canadese* and *Comunita' Viva.*

Evviva L'Italian! Evviva La Colonia!

There is no doubt in the minds of scholars and academics alike that this policy of multiculturalism has played a crucial role in the development of a pluralistic Canadian culture. There are more people in Toronto who can trace their heritage to a country other than Italy than there are residents of Italian ancestry. Toronto offers a mosaic of cultures where Greeks, Chinese, the British, West Indians, Liechtensteinians are all paesani.

Toronto The Good, Toronto The Gay

Michael Howell

Lithe young men holding hands as they wend their way through the streets of their deliciously Bohemian, life-is-a-carnival neighbourhood? That's Castro Street in San Francisco.

Beefcake in leather, lounging provocatively under street lamps on the wild side of town? You'll find that scene on Christopher Street in New York.

Pretty young disco boys chattering like magpies outside garishly lit discos? Try la rue Stanley in Montreal.

None of that here, thank you very much. Only in Toronto could *good* and *gay* wind up in the same sentence. Ditch the bitchy and abandon the stereotypes. In Toronto the homosexual population is talking happy homemaking, conjugal bliss and (yes, Queen Victoria) S-E-X behind closed doors. Even Toronto's 225,000 gays know that discretion is the better part of survival. They too have joined the ranks of Metro minorities united in low profile and slavish devotion to the Protestant Work Ethic.

Follow the rules, do your job and leave work after 5 p.m. and no one cares if you go home with Frank, or for that matter, go out cruising for a Tom, Dick or Harry. Nor will anyone spend much time wondering why Phyllis shortens her name to Phil when she gets home to Mary Jane.

If, like the rest of Toronto the Good, you only do 'It' behind closed doors, you'll be just one of the gang. (Remember, however, that 'It' includes looking, touching, kissing and thinking about.)

Oh sure, there are some visible members of this minority, too. The slender, well-coiffed, manicured laddie with the plucked eyebrows who served you croissants in Yorkville this morning, and the Warren Beatty number who constantly adjusts his padded crotch to keep it from slipping out of sight. But for every one of the flashier numbers there are hundreds of ordinary gay men and women who, after five o'clock, are more likely to throw off pinstripes and overalls and get into softball, pectorals and dinner.

They're the unlikely pumpers of iron (pecs of death are *de rigeur* in certain gay bars) or the puzzled homemaker roaming the aisles of Loblaw's in search of some missing spice. They're off in Rosedale giving dinners for six and talking about problems with the family; you know, the dogs, the cats, the cars. And they belong to the Judy Garland Memorial Bowling League, the Cabbagetown Softball League (for men) and the Salukis League (for women). Or they're among the one hundred proud members of the Toronto Lambda Business Council of gay-owned enterprises. Hardly Sodom and Gommorah, is it?

Expecting the abnormal? Forget it. Especially when prowling through the two dozen bars and discos frequented by the boys and girls. Expecting something racy behind the doors of places with names like Chaps, Boots or Buddy's? You'll get dull, drab and boring. And that's not just the decor. These places exude a predictably understated indifference, with their predictably painted walls of grey, black or bile green, and the exciting atmosphere of a mineshaft.

Buy a copy of *The Body Politic*, Toronto's wonderfully wittily named gay newspaper. But check your sense of humour at the masthead kids. The tone between the covers underlines again and again the importance of being earnest.

If all this leaves you puzzled and less than titillated, imagine what it's doing to the quarter million men and women droning along in the quietude of understatement and boredom. They're doomed to a lower case lifestyle. All of which begs this question: what's the point of coming out of the closet only to end up looking and acting like Beaver Cleaver?

10 Things That Will Never Happen to White People in Toronto

Lillian Allen

• Busted for jay-walking? You'll never be asked for your passport or landed papers.

• No one will ever ask if you have an illegal friend who wants a cleaning job.

• If you work in the courthouse, you'll never be asked "Where's your representative?" when you stand up to represent someone.

• No one will ever assume that you can do the moonwalk.

• No one will ever ask you to recommend an unspoiled beach in Jamaica.

• No one will ever assume you live in the Jane-Finch corridor.

• At parties where grass is circulating freely you'll never be asked where to get the "really good stuff."

• You'll never feel like a raisin in a sponge cake.

• No one will ever assume you're voicing an opinion on behalf of the entire white population of Canada.

• No one will ever tell you to go back where you came from.

Three Places Where Being Black is a Definite Advantage

• Churches with a declining membership

• The police recruitment centre. They're *still* trying to fill a quota.

• Government committees on multiculturalism and visible minorities. (They won't pay you, but they will keep your coffee cup filled.)

Neighbourhood Watch

Ian Pearson

Some days my heart is full: I walk through these streets and exult in the clog-shod children tapping out their step-dances, the graceful women in their saris, the jolly schnitzel vendors in their lederhosen. That's what this city is all about — a never-ending pageant of fascinating folklore and worldly joy, alive and well in the neighbourhoods. Here the colourful Greeks, there the colourful Italians, in between the colourful Portuguese. And it's my job to keep it that way.

Jack Strachan is the name — they call me Strachan-arm Jack — and neighbourhood purification is the game. I work for the Commissioner of Neighbourhoods. We're silent but essential, a top-secret department tucked away in a corner at City Hall where no one ever enters: the mayor's office. Our job is to keep the spirit of the city intact by keeping the neighbourhoods distinctive, preventing them from getting what we call "smudged." We don't want the tourists, or the mayor, to get confused.

Here's what I mean: one day I'm checking out College and Ossington, heart of Little Italy. As I saunter along, I spot a bin of macadamia nuts wedged in between the eggplants and finocchio. You may not find this alarming, but tough experience has taught me the dire truth of the domino theory of imported produce. After the macadamia nuts comes the frozen lamb, then CHIN is playing Men At Work and soon Ossington Avenue is crawling with bloody poms. City Council passes a cute resolution to rename it Aussietown and in no time at all the stallions in the Bar Diplomatico get short-spiky Mel Gibson haircuts and chug Foster's as they practice their sailing knots. That's how a neighbourhood gets "smudged," when the wrong sort of local colour tints its way into the cultural kaleidoscope. I've seen it happen too many times. This case was easy: a surreptitious squirt of Javex on the macadamias and it's "Ciao, ciao, koala."

Now I said some days my heart is full. Those are the days of the fast simple jobs: swiping pesto from a Forest Hill kitchen; abducting a guy with close-cropped hair, mustache, pink tank top and cut-offs (with a Barbara Pym novel in the back pocket) from Leaside and dropping him at Wellesley and Church; outbidding a CBC producer for a house in Scarborough to keep him safely in Cabbagetown; hijacking cases of Kirin beer bound for Danforth; routing anyone with any personality or intellect away from Yorkville.

But on other days my burden is heavy. I feel that the entire city has been smudged so irrevocably that I might as well become a condominium salesman for all the success I'm having in preserving the cultural patchwork. That is how disappointed I felt at the outset of my most difficult case, when I realized that my control over the neighbourhoods was being threatened from within City Hall. As I said, the Commissioner of Neighbourhoods was top secret. In fact, I had never met my boss face-to-face, although I had my suspicions that he might be the Big Boss of the whole place. My instructions were always written on used Caravan passports and slipped under my door. But not long ago my instructions started taking a strange turn in direction.

"Smuggle *Indiana Jones* into the Naaz Cinema" read the first missive, followed shortly by "Set up Burger King at Spadina and Dundas." Finally it was "Draw up plans for a Casino-Hotel on Algonquin Island." The trichina worms were beginning to turn in Hogtown. This wasn't purification, it was full-fledged Calgaryfication, guaranteed to purée the magical Metro mosaic into bland urban mush. My job was to keep people in their merry place, not to relegate them to no-place. So I set out to discover who was out to destroy the neighbourhoods.

In my mind, I constructed the pathology of a man who would want to smash People City. His favourite restaurant would be Ed's Warehouse (he would always be given a tie to wear over his turtleneck);

he would live in North York and drive downtown in a large Chrysler listening to Hagood Hardy on the eight-track; he would be an Argo fan who loved CNE chili dogs; he would own the autographs of Al Waxman, Adam Timoon and Wayne (but not Shuster); his favourite writers would be Robert Ludlum and Gary Lautens (who once smiled at him in a Shopper's Drug Mart). In short, a man allergic to local colour. I shuddered as I realized I recognized my enemy. It had to be the Big Boss himself: only a man with a permanent and a fake jaw would want to wage war on the neighbourhoods.

But I had to confirm it. I deduced that there was only one place that my nemesis would go for an after-work drink; the Troubadour Steakhouse in a mall on Sheppard Avenue, the paradigm of a non-neighbourhood. I quickly stationed myself there and nursed a rye-and-coke (I always go native) as I awaited the arrival of my quarry. Sure enough, just as Scotty MacDonald was beginning his inimitable piano styling of *The Way We Were*, the Big Boss walked through the door. He sat down at the piano bar, ordered a Rob Roy and sat back to relax. Scotty, in an uncharacteristically multi-cultural turn, announced a medley dedicated to the neighbourhoods of Metro: "I'd like to begin, ladies and gentlemen, with a tribute to our Italian neighbours. Here's Umberto Tozzi's *Ti Amo...*"

"NO, NO!" shrieked the Big Boss, "Not here. Not in the last haven of the non-neighbourhood. I want words that I can understand. I want a melody that I would hear in Cleveland Airport. I want houses that don't blind me with garish colours. I want streets where everybody stays inside and minds their own business. I want to know what kind of food I'm ordering and I want it to be meat and potatoes. I want everybody to keep quiet and act the same. I want us all to worship in the same domed stadium. I WANT THIS CITY TO GROW UP!"

He had finally unmasked himself. The clientele of the Troubadour was awestruck as I escorted him to the waiting paddy-wagon. The affair was, of course, hushed up and city administrators shuffled off the Big Boss to a meaningless job on a newspaper, ensuring that he would remain powerless in future.

As for me, I'm still on the beat, keeping things vibrant and unique. You may pass me on the street as I stealthily approach my next assignment. And you'll point with pride at Strachan-arm Jack as you boast to your fellow citizens, "There goes the neighbourhood."

MILDRED PORRIDGE-MONARCHIST

ACTUALLY THE WILLOWDALE CHAPTER OF THE MONARCHIST LEAGUE WAS HOPING THAT IT WOULDN'T HAVE TO SEND 'OLD MILDRED' TO LONDON AGAIN FOR THE LATEST ROYAL WEDDING. BUT, WHAT WITH HER CONSTANT LOBBYING, PAMPHLET-EERING, THREATENED HUNGER-STRIKES AND LETTER-BOMBS, IT WAS DECIDED TO LET HER GO. BESIDES, THE TERRORIST SQUAD OF THE R.C.M.P. WAS RAPIDLY BUILDING A FILE ON HER AS THICK AS YOUR FIST!

YORK SQUADRON ROYAL AIR FORCE

VIRTUE IS MY HELMET!!

AISLIN 81

GREAT GREASE
LES NIRENBERG

For a while in the late forties, my kid brother and I were the only Jewish kids at Davenport Road Public School in the West End of Toronto. Our faces and bikes were regularly trashed by toughs with Scottish and English names whose fathers worked for the TTC, John Inglis, Swifts, Canada Packers or any of the depressing industries in what later came to be known as the Junction Triangle. These bullies had other victims too. They were the kids who lived in a small enclave that stretched roughly from Landsdowne Avenue in the east, to Keele Street in the west, and between St. Clair and Davenport Road.

Their parents often said they were Greek, but they didn't speak Greek. Later on I was to find out most of them were slavic Macedonians. They came from a country that no longer existed. It had been divvied up among Greece, Bulgaria and Yugoslavia. But in Toronto in the forties and fifties they were alive and well, and a force to be reckoned with. Why? Because they owned most of the neighbourhood greasy spoons. They worked long, hard hours and dished out massive menus of chips, hot chicken, turkey and beef sandwiches drowned in a thick brown concoction they called gravy. Everything tasted the same, and came with mashed potatoes and peas and carrots scooped from huge institutional cans. You could actually watch the cook making the toasted Western, the gravy and the rice pudding.

When people recall the old Toronto, they often talk about "banks and churches" on every corner. Well, the Macedonian restaurant was the institution in the middle of the block. Today it's seldom mentioned. Neither is the old time English fish and chip store. Canadian soldiers back from the War brought this business to Toronto with them. The neighbourhood fish and chip store was where my school-boy enemies usually hung out. But it was worth the risk to latch on to the great greasy hand-cut fries soaked in vinegar and piled into a cone made out of yesterday's Tely. Those chips were GOOD! So was the fish. Not the gefilte kind my mother made, but great fluffy lumps of halibut covered in a crispy coating, that oozed hot crankcase fluid when you bit into them. They used beef drippings, not vegetable oil, to fry the stuff in, and the smell would linger in your clothes for days. Later on I was to discover the devastating effect all of this had on my gall bladder.

Well, the days of the Macedonian restaurant are over. Gone too are the old fish and chip shops. Toronto has become a gourmet paradise where you have to lay out hundreds of dollars for a good steak, or a fancy plate of organ meats served in a fern garden.

Well, amongst those high-priced fancy places, the little boites run by aging hippies doling out carrot cake, and the California-style burger joints with their tasteless beef in a basket and fries with cute names like "Meadow Muffins," you can still find the Great Grease of Toronto. Take the time to search them out. And if you find any, please tell me so I can add them to my personal scrap book of Great Grease.

BAGEL WORLD
336 Wilson Avenue

Get off the westbound 401 at Bathurst and you'll find yourself face-to-face with what looks like a gigantic human breast. Don't let this rattle you. It's actually the front sign of Bagel World.

Inside, two ex-prize-fighters, brothers named Bill and Peter Zaduk, will sell you lox, cheeses, eggs and other goodies to pile on top of one of the tastiest bagels in Toronto. "We get everybody in here," says Peter, "from the people who run the country to the people who run it down." On good days you'll meet Bob Kaplan, Sammy Luftspring, Wayne and Shuster and the funniest, and smartest collection of taxi drivers and rounders in town. Go ahead, butt into the conversations. Everybody does. See if you can match wits on sports or politics. When you leave, destroyed by their wisecracks, take a dozen bagels home for the freezer.

BARNEY'S
385 Queen Street West

This is no place for a lingering lunch. There are only thirteen stools at the counter and seats for nine people at the postage-stamp tables. You have to eat it and beat it, so don't be insulted if Barney Devore asks you to make tracks. What attracts everyone from the Plutocrats to the Punkers is a good corned beef and a dynamite breakfast. Ask septuagenarian Barney how he's done it for the past thirty-five years and he'll show you the write-up he got in the New York Times. But don't linger. He needs the seat for the next customer.

THE EATING COUNTER
41 Baldwin Street

When Joe Chan and Charlie Ng opened the Eating Counter four years ago, it was half the size it is now. Charlie did all the cooking in an open kitchen area. The place was constantly filled with smoke from their flambé dishes. Rosedale and Forest Hill matrons had to go home after the meal to shower and change clothes to get the smoke and grease out. Diefenbachia plants on the counter dripped cooking oil. Now the eating area is separate from the cooking area, but you can still watch Charlie in action through an open door. He moves like a ballet dancer, slicing, dicing, whisking the food in a giant wok over a volcano of fire that roars four or five feet into the air. The cooking is a mix of Cantonese, Szechuan and Malaysian, with MSG just about eliminated. Seafood and barbecue, along with their sizzling pots and flaming dishes are excellent and fun. If you're game, ask Joe about his Snake Soup.

CAMARRA'S PIZZA
2899 Dufferin Street

Elisabetta Valentini has been running Camarra's Pizza since 1958. (It was Toronto's first sit-down pizzeria.) Back then the place was an Italian bakery. Pizza made from her mother's recipe was a sideline. Soon the demand for pizza was so heavy that Elisabetta had to phase out the pastries and concentrate on pizza. Her secret is a yeast-based dough that's light and soft and even tastes delicious when it's cold. I tried to pry the recipe out of one of her gorgeous daughters, Diana, but gave up when she said, "If I told, grandma would kill me."

YUNG SING PASTRY SHOP
22 Baldwin Street

Ko Chu and his wife Ko Ngan have been running this little bakery since they came here from Hong Kong in 1968. They sell about 1,000 meat-filled and sweet Chinese buns a day, and the same amount in Dim Sum on the weekends. A fistful of lunch consisting of a curry turnover and a spring roll will cost you about $1.10. This is a favourite place for kids from the student ghetto, nurses and doctors from neighbouring hospitals, and surrounding Chinatown.

The line-up outside this former kosher butcher shop reaches well out into the street at lunchtime. When you get to the counter, remember the Kos don't speak English, so you have to point at what you want.

LOH'S
2368A Yonge Street

The Loh family made hand-cranked ice-cream with salt and ice back in New Zealand. Then they moved to Kingston, Jamaica, and perfected their recipes, incorporating a lot of exotic West Indian and South American fruits. Just over two years ago they came to Toronto and sprang their ice-cream on Canadians. Their little basement store has a machine in the window that makes all their ice-cream, five gallons at a time. Flavours include mango, coconut, lychee, ginger and a South American fruit called guarana. If you ask them what Chinese people are doing making and selling ice-cream they'll remind you that Marco Polo brought the stuff to Italy and the World, but that the Chinese started it all.

MARS
432 College Street

Mars is a favourite spot for taxi drivers in search of good solid food at a low price. In 1974 Sam and Eugene Kristy took a giant step for mankind when they invented the famous Mars Muffin. These hummungus creations come in blueberry, corn or bran, and have kept Mars regulars regular since the boys started baking them with their secret recipe. The place is a favourite for show-biz celebrities like Bruce Cockburn, lawyers like Eddy Greenspan. Suzanne Somers and Al Hamel stock up on muffins, or their huge runny butter tarts, whenever they're here on a visit from L.A.

PENROSE FISH & CHIPS
600 Mount Pleasant Road

The old fish and chips stores that choked Toronto streets back in the forties and fifties are gone, but a hearty few still exist and still deliver the genuine article. Roland Johnston opened this place after spending the war years in London. He's now in semi-retirement, and the little place is run by his wife Marion, his son David and a small dedicated army of fish fryers. They use classic beef drippings here, and the Penrose gang spend the early morning hours each day filleting halibut, and cutting fries, and mixing their secret batter. Thirty-five years ago, Roland Johnston recalls, an order was fifteen cents and chips alone were a nickel. Now an order is $2.70 and solo chips eighty-five cents.

SAN FRANCESCO
10 Clinton Street

Mike and Anna Pimpinella bought San Francesco from founder Vincenzo Saudia in 1983. There are eight San Francescos around Toronto, but the Clinton Street address is where it all started twenty-seven years ago. And this is where the Pimpinella's hearts are. Huge salamis, mortadellas and cheeses crowd the tiny neighbourhood grocery store. Parking here is a horror, as locals, Argos, Italian entertainers, politicians and people from Johnny Lombardi's ethnic radio station elbow each other for veal, sausage and meatball sandwiches. They come in three categories: hot, hotter and hottest. Once you have your sandwich, take it to the beer parlour next door.

MOE PANCER
4130 Bathurst Street

Moe Pancer is a motor-mouth, but he makes a helluva pastrami. Ditto for corned beef and baby beef. Moe also carries my favourite soft drink: Vernor's, the best ginger ale in the world. His clients consume about a ton of meat every week, and that's not counting the borscht, the salads, the dumplings and the rest of the stuff that adds inches to my ass every time I look at it.

Ask Moe about his philosophy and he'll tell you: "I'm the Greatest." This Muhammad Ali of Meat has shipped his briskets to Israel, Mexico, Calgary and Texas. He even got an order from the Minister of Trade of Haiti. Moe's ambition is to be able to produce a good quality, low price rib steak for his clientele. Good luck Moe!

Photographer: Russ Forfar

A NEWCOMER'S QUIZ

You! Newcomer!
Think you can cut it in T.O.?
Answer these questions and we'll see! (Please?)

1. Who sold the site of Toronto to the British for £1,700, plus assorted goods?

a) Century 21
b) the Mississauga Indians
c) Timothy Eaton

2. Honest Ed is

a) Ed Mirvish
b) Ed Broadbent
c) Ed Sullivan
d) Mr. Ed

3. What is the longest running street in the world?

a) Coronation Street
b) Sesame Street
c) Yonge Street

4. What features a dramatic 300 foot sheer drop?

a) the CN Tower
b) the Canadian dollar
c) the Scarborough Bluffs

5. "Poop and Scoop" is

a) a new flavour of ice-cream
b) a dog-owner's pastime
c) a communist conspiracy

6. The Reichmann Brothers are

a) a circus act
b) owners of a construction company
c) country singers

7. ROM is

a) the Royal Ontario Museum
b) Jamaican rum
c) a male Gypsy

8. Where did MacKenzie's rebels gather in 1837?

a) Winston's
b) Maple Leaf Gardens
c) Montgomery's Tavern

9. Who gave Toronto its real name (not Fort Rouillé, not York, not Hogtown, but . . .)

a) God
b) the Huron Indians
c) Frederick G. Gardiner

10. The Maple Leafs are

a) a hockey team
b) junior botanists
c) a joke
d) all of the above

— 68 —

11. Joe Pantalone is

a) an Italian lingerie salesman
b) a Toronto alderman
c) a hit man

12. What were the leading families of Toronto society called?

a) the Argus Corp.
b) the Family Compact
c) The Band
d) a situation comedy

13. Rough Trade is

a) a new wave band
b) the Toronto Stock Exchange
c) an afternoon on Yonge Street

14. Kiss and Ride is

a) a suburban kiss-off
b) a gay rodeo
c) an accident looking for somewhere to happen

15. Put in chronological order

a) the crash of 1929
b) the Rebellion of 1837
c) the War of 1812
d) Pope John Paul the Second

16. Explain the following phenomena

a) Gibralter Point
b) Scarborough Bluffs
c) Hogg's Hollow
d) homosexuality

17. The windows of the Royal Bank building contain

a) 1.2 million dollars
b) fool's gold
c) glass
d) all of the above

18. The 20-Minute Workout is

a) a laxative
b) new math
c) a trendy exercise show

19. Who's famous for their massive facades?

a) Barbara Amiel
b) The Toronto Argonauts
c) The University of Toronto

20. Which of these street names is regularly mispronounced?

a) Yonge
b) St. Catherine
c) Spadina
d) Balliol

Answers

1. "B" (1 point) Easy question — that's all it's worth.

2. "A" (1 point) Ditto. Minus 10 if you missed it.

3. "C" (2 points) Yonge Street wins in distance but if you guessed "A" minus 5 points (Snap out of it, we're in the 20th century).

4. "C" (2 points) (What the hell — take 2 points for any answer.)

5. "B" (2 points) — if you guessed "C" deduct 2 points for paranoia.

6. "B" (1 point — we have only their word for it that they're not "A" or "C")

7. "C" (5 points) Yes! Look it up in the Oxford! Deduct 2 points if you guessed "A." Over-enthusiasm gets you nothing here.

8. "C" (3 points) However, it burned to the ground in the 1880s.

9. "B" (2 points) but if you rejected "C" because you knew he was Metro Toronto's first Chairperson, give yourself 5 points (Smartass!).

10. Does it really matter? Diehards can award themselves 1 point for any answer.

11. "B" (3 points) If you answered "C" shame on you — he's such a nice guy.

12. "B" (2 points) but 1 point for "D."

13. "A" (2 points) If you answered "B" give yourself a point, but only if you're a stockbroker.

14. "A" (2 points) If you guessed "B" you obviously don't live in suburbia.

15. Give yourself 5 points if you even attempted this one.

16. Gibralter Point: the tip of the sandbar forming the Toronto harbour (2 points); Scarborough Bluffs: a geographic record of glacial ages (2 points); Hogg's Hollow: the location of Montgomery's Tavern (2 points); Homosexuality: oh, come on, do we have to tell you everything?

17. "D" but no points — who cares anyway.

18. "C" (2 points) Add an extra 5 points if you do it every morning.

19. "C" (2 points) for the staid — the innovative may give themselves 1 point for either of the other answers.

20. "C" (5 points) It was named after a man who pronounced his name *Spadeena*. An extra point if you caught the ringer and an extra five if you have the foggiest idea about "D." We don't.

What Your Score Means

46 — 66: Congratulations — you are now officially a member of the Toronto establishment. Peter C. Newman will be contacting you shortly.

21 — 45: Well, hello Mr. or Ms. Average! You'll never make it to the legislature but you know what you need to know. You'll fit right in.

0 — 20: Oh dear. Perhaps Calgary . . . or Buffalo . . .

METRO LIFE

Remember this . . .
in Toronto, Lifestyle is everything.

TUPPYS
Toronto Urban Professionals

Karen Flanagan-McCarthy

Tuppy: n. *Toronto Urban Professional: Any individual born during the baby boom who, after years of "fighting the establishment" and flirting with socialism, has discovered that capitalism is where it's at and that upwardly mobile is the only way to go.*

DO YOU:
- Get home delivery of the Sunday *New York Times*?
- Drive a Volvo, Saab or Subaru?
- Own a VCR, personal computer or microwave oven?
- Belong to a health club and/or play squash regularly?
- Have a financial counsellor, therapist and/or cleaning lady?
- Have a wine cellar?

If you answered yes to any three of those questions, you are a Tuppy. Don't try to hide it, and don't be embarrassed. In Toronto, making money (lots of it) is nothing to be ashamed of. Especially in a city with a church named after Timothy Eaton. Worshipping the almighty (though devalued) dollar is truly a religion here. If you've got it, flaunt it. If you don't, charge it.

Still, it must be done discreetly and in the approved manner, cafés and neighbourhoods, and with the right sort of people, using the appropriate terminology. Read along if you have even the slightest doubt.

For a Tuppy, appearance is everything. Nothing, from the pen you use to your choice of groceries, is inconsequential. You must learn to walk, talk, dress, live, eat, drink, think, spell, see, appreciate and congregate with insouciance.

Tupperwear

Expensive suits, slacks, shirts and blouses in raw silk, wool or linen.

Creeds, Brogue and David's are in. Marks and Spencer is OK for panty hose. The Bay is definitely out. Someone might recognize your outfit from the supplement in last week's newspaper. Simpson's is also out, unless you're shopping for designer threads in The Room. Shop at Sportables for that weekend "preppie" look.

Don't go the budget basement route when clothing yourself. Remember, clothes are simply another necessary investment.

A Tuppy Shopping Tip: Carry credit cards from Sak's, Lord and Taylor and Bonwit Teller. Keep them in your wallet next to the Gold American Express Card. Give the Bloomingdale's card to your little sister.

Tupperwhere

Tuppys avoid neighbourhoods which are still too ethnic to be considered chic. *Chic* is sandblasted buildings; *ethnic* is pastel-coloured houses with the bricks outlined in white.

Preferred neighbourhoods are as simple as ABC: the Annex, the Beaches, Cabbagetown. Definitely out are highrises in Davisville, any suburb that was farmland before WWII and any neighbourhood without a decent Italian restaurant. Certain areas of Parkdale are considered a near-miss.

Your home must, of course, be tasteful . . . decorated either in austere hi-tech or cozy antique. Pine is out, oak is in. Rooms are usually painted white. A good stereo (in black or dull grey) is a must and posters must be framed. Stained-glass windows are a nice touch, but only if they're old and hand-leaded. Post-war stained glass is a dead giveaway that you grew up in the suburbs.

You are encouraged to explain to your guests the lengths to which you went to get the place looking just so. Comparing Italian and Dutch tilework will demonstrate your *bona fides,* as will a discussion of kitchen designs. Avoid knowing anything about plumbing lest the conversation descend to the level of counter chatter at a Beaver outlet.

A Nice Touch: Artfully strewn copies of *Architectural Digest* on an IKEA coffee table.

Tuppertoys

Most of these will be found in the kitchen. Even though you won't really have time to cook (except on weekends and special occasions), you should have the machinery on hand to whip up dinner for 12 in a snap.

Give yourself five points for each of the following:
- a Cuisinart (with every blade ever made)
- a pasta machine
- an ice cream and/or yogurt maker
- a microwave oven
- a crepe maker
- a wok (electric doesn't count)
- an omelette pan (extra points if you've ever thrown one out because some boor actually washed it)
- an espresso machine (must have the steam spout for cappucino)
- a sprout farmer (very popular with Tuppys from back-to-the-land backgrounds)
- a compact disc player
- a personal computer (extra points if you use it)
- a VCR (extra points if you don't have x-rated movies)
- a telephone answering machine
- a bidet
- a jacuzzi attachment for your tub
- a 35 mm camera with an underwater casing

Tuppertalk

Of course there's a jargon you'll want to learn if you're serious about social success. How else does one keep out the parvenus?

Tuppertalk is rooted in French, Yiddish, computerese, 60's slang and of course, English. It's not really all that hard to learn, but do be careful that you use it appropriately. A minor slip, especially in the Yiddish expressions, could have serious consequences.

Feedback: Opinions (usually someone else's, usually unwelcome). Can be used as a stalling technique, as in "We should get the client's feedback on this."

Gentrify: See Tupperwhere

Input: Ideas (again, often someone else's). Can be helpful when working on tedious projects, as in "I think Brophy's input would be valuable here."

Interface: To engage in meaningful dialogue with persons or computers.

Network: Something you should be doing with as many people as possible. If you don't know the meaning of this word, perhaps you're not really a Tuppy.

Pencil You In: Something you will have after networking. As in daybook; something subtle and leather which you should have with you at all times. (Hint: not a good phrase to use in conversation with the boss.) This phrase is most often preceded by "Let me check my book."

Tuppys also like abbreviations, as in "S.O." (Significant Other). Your S.O. is not necessarily your spouse, but could be. "L.T.R."(Long-Term Relationship) is another popular abbreviation in Tuppy circles. L.T.R. can be used to describe your S.O., but your S.O. may not be an L.T.R. Only you can decide this.

Other abbreviations to use in casual conversation:

A.G.O.	*Never* say the Art Gallery of Ontario
RHOSP	pronounce this one "R-Hosp." This is something every Tuppy aspiring to home owner- ship has.
T.O.	Where you live, when talking with outsiders.

Elementary Yiddish

Very important in media, advertising or "entertainment circles." This comes from watching too many Woody Allen films, and has led to some incongruities such as Deirdre McGee saying "It's to die for . . ." (as in a $1,000 dress from Creeds).

Kibbitz:	To chat or gossip. Not to be confused with kibbutz, a place no self-respecting Tuppy would work.
Dreck:	Cheap or worthless objects: things Tuppys would never own.
Yenta:	A gossipy woman; e.g., your Aunt Matilda who never tires of asking when you're going to get serious and find a suitable mate to settle down with.
Shmooze:	A friendly, gossipy chat: an integral part of networking.
Boychik:	Separate the syllables and what have you got? Something every female Tuppy should have in her life. Get 'em young and train 'em early.
Chazer:	A pig, an ingrate, someone who is cheap or stingy; someone who invites you to lunch at his/her club and doesn't pick up the tab.
Nebbish:	The early Woody Allen; a jerk, a nerd. Someone who'd take his mother on a Club Med vacation.
Frum:	The family name of one of "*The Journal*" co-hosts. When properly pronounced in Yiddish (froom), means religious or orthodox, which Barbara may or may not be. Ask her.

Tuppolitik

The heady days of the 60s are almost twenty years behind you. Still, you may suffer the odd guilt twinge as you try to reconcile today's quotes from Wall street with yesterday's quotes from Marx.

Twinge no more. Follow these simple guidelines and you'll pre-empt any talk of "selling out."

- Drive a Swedish car.
- Vacation in Cuba or Nicaragua. Express horror at the very idea of Club Med in Haiti.
- Pay your cleaning lady or nanny *more* than the going rate. This way you can never be accused of Third World exploitation.
- Give money to worthy causes. (This can be less painful than you may think. Many good causes are tax deductible.)
- Know a starving artist. Take him/her to lunch once in a while. (Write it off on the expense account.)
- March in at least one demo a year. (Anti-nuke is the safe bet.)
- Subscribe to *This Magazine* and *Mother Jones*.
- If you're really committed (and don't have lots of capital) buy a house in a co-op with one or two friends. (This can look suspicious if you buy four or more houses.)
- Prefer *The Return of the Secaucus Seven* to *The Big Chill*.
- Keep a small supply of top quality grass on hand for serious bouts of nostalgia.

Tupperlove

Maybe it's fear of herpes and/or AIDS, but monogamy (even serial) is definitely on the rise. Many Tuppys are looking for that certain someone with whom they can share their lives and tax deductions.

"...BUT THEN, EVERY ONCE IN AWHILE, I FANTASIZE ABOUT BEING BAREFOOT AND PREGNANT."

Do's and Don'ts For Male Tuppys

- Show her how capable you are. Sew on a button (not at the collar) in the taxi on the way to dinner.
- Show her you're serious about food; keep copies of *Gourmet* or *Bon Appetit* in the bathroom; know the names of three French chefs; cook dinner for her. (This is easier than it sounds; just get mom or the cleaning lady to whip up something ethnic that you can re-heat.)
- Let her know that you believe that birth control is a shared responsibility. Drop tantalizing hints that you're thinking about a vasectomy. In the meantime, spring for a new IUD.
- Don't assume you'll be spending the night if she invites you in for a nightcap. Wait for an invitation.
- Don't wear gold chains or drive American sports cars.
- Don't refer to women as chicks, broads, or even girls. This will mark you as a man in need of too much re-education to be of much interest.

Do's and Don'ts For Female Tuppys

- Show him how capable you are. Change the washer on that dripping faucet in the bathroom.
- Show him you're serious about business: keep copies of *Fortune* and *Forbes* in the kitchen; know the names of three up-and-coming-hi-tech stocks; invite him over for an appraisal of his insurance needs. (This is easier than it sounds: get your mom or your agent to do it for you.)

Q: What Makes Torontonians Laugh?
A: Allan Gould

People speak of Irish humour; of Jewish wit; of Toronto half-wit. But never before has a list of specifically Torontonian jokes been excavated, organized, collated and listed — with commentary.

Here they are, then: jokes, ribald classics (these are cracks which go back almost a decade), gags, and one-liners. All culled at great expense and time-consumption from bars and dinner tables from Mimico to Newmarket, university classrooms from the University of Toronto to York — the latter a joke in itself — high school cafeterias, and bathroom walls (this could eliminate Scarborough, which has yet to install indoor plumbing in most homes). Read 'em an' laugh. Torontonians do!!

Q . How many Torontonians does it take to change a
     lightbulb?
A . In Rosedale, the butler does it. In North York, the
     husband; in Little Italy, a professional carpenter who is also
     the husband; in Scarborough, they wouldn't notice that it
     was out until it was dark outside, and by then, they'd all
     be asleep anyway!!!

(COMMENT: This joke with its acerbic and pointed satire on the various geographic areas of the city with their variant economic, cultural and social milieus, is always greeted by Torontonians with gales of laughter. Even if they have heard it before. Especially if they have heard it before.)

Harry: When is a Blue Jay player like a thief?
Larry: When he steals a base!!!

(COMMENT: This witticism is only enjoyed by Torontonians who are familiar with their professional baseball club, the Toronto Blue Jays. But those who "get it" often chuckle for long minutes, showing the healthy attitude that the people have toward the "sporting life." Some commentators feel that this generous response has more to do with the sale of beer in the ball park, something which Torontonians have been able to experience only since the mother of the premier, William Grenville Davis, passed away.)

Question: What can you do with a dead cat?
Torontonian: Why, you shouldn't do anything with it. It should be buried at once!!

(COMMENT: Terrific gags like this one underline the profound moral sense of Torontonians. There is nothing funny about a dead cat, and the Torontonian is the sort of person who cannot joke about such things. Indeed, dead cats can spread disease, and some little kid who owned the poor cat is probably broken-hearted. No one can quite explain why Torontonians have such a deep moral sensibility, as well as such a great wit; some feel it has something to do with being ruled by the same political party for over 500 years.)

A Torontonian asked a man (who hailed from Regina) where he was from.
"Saskatchewan," he replied.
"Bless you!!" said the Torontonian.

(COMMENT: This kind of playful jabbing at our friends from the prairies is a common one, heard everywhere on the streets of Toronto. Someone once figured out why this charming rivalry exists between the two provinces, but we think he died. Or was it she?)

Jerry: How do you make antifreeze?
Mary: You steal her blanket!!

(COMMENT: A perennial favourite, heard on nearly every street corner of Toronto, but only during the winter, which usually lasts from just after Labour Day until mid-May.)

Roman Catholic Separate School Teacher: "Johnny, if you were facing the North Pole and Manitoba was on your left, what would be on your right?
Johnny: My hockey stick!!

(COMMENT: Heard frequently in the early 1980s, usually in singles bars, and wherever "macho men" hang out. Yet also common on Bay Street, surprisingly. Not only is the keen wit of Torontonians underlined in this joke, but their tolerance for ethnic groups (it is after all an R.C. teacher). Note too their great love for winter sports.)

Toronto Husband: How do you spell "Ontario?"
Toronto Wife: The Province or the Lake?

(COMMENT: Admittedly, an example of Toronto sexist humour, often heard in more ethnic areas, although surprisingly common on Bay Street. Shockingly, a growing number of Toronto women have begun to tell this story with the roles reversed, which suggests an explosion of feminism not seen before 1982.)

A tanned tourist went up to Muskoka,
Couldn't swim — but she *did* know the Polka!
She danced everywhere
Until chased by a bear
She's no longer the colour of mocha

(COMMENT: God, we're still giggling over this one. But to the point: this was without a doubt the most popular limerick of the past decade. Torontonians, for some reason, are obsessed with limericks, and tell them to one another by dozens every day. This one, to be frank, is a bit more risqué and violent than most. In fact we were begged by three different groups not to include it in this book, but we ignored them, since it is such a classic example. They include Mary Brown, of the Ontario Censor Board (for its violence), Contrast, the black newspaper (for its racism, and suggestions that only tourists are dark, or that skin colour can be removed in that fashion), and the Ontario Board for the Status of Women (sexism — why couldn't it have been a male who was eaten by the bear?). Marion Engel, on the other hand, asked for royalties.
It is rare when a single joke (limerick or otherwise) could offend so many Torontonians, and this clearly shows how deeply the citizens feel about this sort of thing. But God, it is funny, isn't it?)

Finally, the best of the lot:

Don: What Canadian animals are still found in Toronto
     banks?
John: The buck and the doe!!

*(COMMENT: Although the second pun of the wonderful punchline (doe —
dough, get it?), nearly always has to be explained to one's fellow Torontonians,
this one is a favourite with the "in crowd." I personally have heard it in Hazelton
Lanes, the Courtyard Café, The Room (Simpsons), Creeds, the York Club, and
so on. With three and often four banks on every street corner of the city, it's
not surprising that this one is a winner.)*

Freud (who was not a Torontonian, by the way) has pointed out
to us just how important and subtle jokes can be. They provide great
insight into a man, a woman, a culture, a religion, a nationality.

Torontonians are a highly complex people, with a sharply defined
sense of humour, as can be seen from the above. From Ben Wicks to
the *Globe and Mail's* Morning Smile, these are a people rich in satire,
parody, wit and good humour.

Long may they laugh.

Painting the Town

John Burgess

Where to go?

What to wear?

These, dear friends, are thorny questions in the Big Lemon. You can't just sleepwalk through your closet and throw on any old Wayne Clark. That's far too spontaneous for this ol' anal retentive burg.

You must plan ahead.

At the O'Keefe Centre, that charming barn that beer built, big tartan skirts and shawls that double as piano covers will do the trick. So will peau-de-soie shoes . . . they go so well with off-white complexions. For matinées, the democratic approach is *de rigeur* (but should be *mortis*): half the house is dressed like survivors of a rug riot at Sears, the other half looking like an explosion in the ski jacket department at Woolco. You'll recognize the Liberace crowd by the smell — polyester and mothballs.

If you're ready for safety pins in your ears, try neo-punk watering holes like the Bam Boo Club on Queen West. But never say "punk" here. The preferred term is "Third World reggae."

Wear steel-toed boots to rock shows at Maple Leaf Gardens. Not for the show, silly. For kicking garbage cans up and down Yonge Street afterwards.

Gentlemen who prefer blondes only if the blondes are also gentlemen are directed to The Quest on Yonge Street. It has a rather lively main floor stand-up lounge, although it does verge on being a wrinkle bar. That's a place frequented by gentlemen who have given up Second Debut and are now using Polyfilla to chase away the pesky crow's feet.

Katrina's is a dance bar just off Yonge Street that is filled with fluffy men and even fluffier boys who engage in heated conversations about the merits of pink versus powder blue angora as a suitable material for tank tops.

Dress for success? Yes, yes, yes! And keep a sharp eye on your role models for fashion guidelines. Conrad Black, for instance, has the clout to wear suits with lapels wide enough to land a 747. Mayor Art Eggleton doesn't. So he leans to (gasp!) brown suits. Can leather knickers be far behind? Paul Godfrey, ex-chairman of Metropolitan Toronto, now publisher of the *Toronto Sun*, gets dressed in a dark closet. His pearl-grey tuxedo makes him look like an usher at Roy Thompson Hall. Fashion-conscious media-types take their cues from Barbara Frum and Mary Lou Finlay — and then beetle off in the opposite direction. Vicious gossip insists that there is really a memo from the CBC wardrobe department which claims "the girls look sharp [sic] in ruffles."

Food, despite rumours to the contrary, is still pedestrian in Toronto. We read about raddicchio and sweetbread soufflés but we order shrimp cocktails and well-done steaks. Toronto's culinary heartland is found at The Toronto, The National and The York clubs in endless variations on consommé, roast beef and Stilton cheese, served up by grandmotherly waitresses who learned grim at Murray's. Way up town at The Granite Club (which must be in another area code if not another time zone), the ladies-who-lunch do sometimes indulge in a little *gratin dauphinois* but in WASP beige only.

Then there's the House of Chan, the favourite Chinese restaurant of Toronto's Jewish community. A consortium of businessmen bought the place because it was losing money and they were looking for a write-off. Sad to say, it suffered an immediate turnaround and has been doing turn-away business ever since. Of course, like the late lamented Ruby Foo's in Montreal, no one, but no one goes to the House of Chan for Chinese food. It's steak and lobster all the way.

For Sunday brunching it's Bregman's on Yonge near St. Clair. The less chi-chi go to the Bagel on College, nicknamed the Dirty Bagel.

Never eat at Winston's. Sit, yes. Eat, no. They will deny it to their dying breath, but the captains of industry (and their admiring chronicler, Peter See) are only there to see and be seen. The last real dish in the place was John Turner.

If the glare off the blue rinse has kept you away from the traditional T.O. eateries, join the I'm-thinking-about-a-career ladies-who-lunch at Il Posto or Fenton's. You're within credit card tossing distance of Bloor Street's Mink Mile, and the portions (not to mention the waiters) are scrumptiously tiny.

Diehards insist that Café Yoo Who, the Courtyard Café, will rise again. Don't bet on it. The only true believers left in the place are the orthodontists who invested in the tax-deductible Canadian movies being concocted before their very eyes at the next table. These orthodontists now spend their weekends trekking out to the boonies to count the house at one of the irregular showings of "I Was A Bilingual Teenage Werewolf." During the week they gather at the Courtyard to discuss the special root-canal procedures they're developing for the producers of that epic

Typical Toronto cuisine? Montreal smoked meat, Buffalo chicken wings, California roll sushi, New York steaks, Yorkshire pudding and spaghetti bolognese. Sliced chicken breast on white bread with mayo is highly regarded and served in ethnic quarters of the city only.

The WASPs of Rosedale are really quite invisible. They have their wooded enclave a stone's throw from the Mink Mile where they purr around the curving streets and charming cul-de-sacs in owned, not leased, Jags and Mercedes. Eccentrics sometimes opt for public transit which is why the Rosedale subway station is free of graffiti, buskers, and panhandlers. TTC conductors have been commanded to roll rather than roar in and out of that particular station — out of respect for the very quiet and quite aged money in residence nearby.

Once a year Rosedale does show its true and gawdy colours at the annual Rosedale-Moore Park Mayfair. Men wear jackets and pants that are loud to the point of cacophony. Ladies don chapeaux festooned with daisies and Venus fly-traps. One Bay Street stalwart even drags out his Davy Crockett hat year after year. Can hula hoops be far behind?

There is life — sort of — out by the airport. Anyone who lives in a town named after a snake (ever heard of the Mississauga rattler?) deserves a fuzzy pink drink called a Jet Stream and a singles bar called Paws.

Some Torontonians (and we know who you are) are attempting to turn Exhibition Park into a hot spot. Cheering. Waving. Speaking louder than a whisper. These people are largely dillettantes; johnny-and-janie-come-latelies who expect pasta and a little green salad between innings. Real Exhibition Park types, male and female, perm their hair in tight little curls and wear oversized nylon windbreakers decorated with many, many chenille crests. Their sons and daughters drag their knuckles when they walk and bellow ''Arrrrrr-gos!!''

What to do? Well, there's Arty Hall, and Massey Hall, and the O'Keefe, and the Royal Alex, and the St. Lawrence Centre, but as every real Torontonian knows, a Saturday night is just not complete without a cruise along Yonge Street. The sound-of-body, strong-of-heart set (usually well over 6'5'' and 240 lbs) saunter down the lower reaches of the Strip, exchanging insults with the lads in Trans-Ams and Firebirds stuck in traffic. Those of a more sensible disposition prefer the northern reaches of the Strip where the worst one can expect is the odd salesman in from Cleveland asking where the action is. Appropriate attire at both ends is a Blue Jays baseball cap (Canadian Tire is an acceptable substitute) and jeans with the cuffs rolled up.

The alternative is to join the sophisticates who spend hours in movie line-ups each and every Saturday night.

What the heck. It beats staying home and taking a bath.

A Day in the Life of
The Sun

Worthington Creighton

A.M.

5:17	Sun rises.
5:21	Security guards arrive to patrol parking lot.
5:37	Security guard puts quarter into red Sun box.
5:38	Security guard puts another quarter in the box.
5:39	Security guard kicks box in and gets Sun.
5:55	Security guard clocks in and goes to bathroom to read Sun.
7:00	Security guard washes ink off his hands.
7:12	Tanker truck of coloured ink arrives for tomorrow's ad supplement.
7:18	Overnight man types long memo to day staff to prove he was there.
8:15	Sun switchboard opens.
8:16	First loon of the day phones looking for Dunford.
8:30	Bonokoski and Dunford go through interoffice mail before mail guy arrives.
8:45	Mail guy takes memos away, but Bono has xeroxed the most interesting.
9:00	Editors begin to arrive.
9:15	Editors read memos to see if they are still editors.
9:18	Sun computer system crashes.
9:30	Morning anti-communism seminar begins.
9:45	Barbara Amiel's secretaries arrive and put down path of rose petals to elevator.
10:00	Nifty designer flak jackets delivered to editor from Creeds.
10:12	Made in Nicaragua labels discovered in flak jackets.
10:18	Jackets returned by courier with stern note.
10:25	Cartoonist Andy Donato begins work on tomorrow's cartoon.
10:31	Editor Amiel wake-up call.
10:38	Donato completes cartoon.
10:45	Communist invasion drill in hardhats, all hands.
11:10	Amiel coffee pot plugged in.

11:12	Amiel's secretary phones Hamilton to see if *Fighting Words* taping today.
11:20	Amiel exec assistants arrive to proof-read William Buckley.
11:45	Editors meet to consider morning possibilities for tomorrow's front:

18 Dead in Lover's Quarrel
Pet Implicated in Death Coven
Dief Alive: Scarborough Psychic

11:48	Bell Canada man arrives to change phone extensions of yesterday's executives.
11:55	Amiel arrives!
11:58	*Front Page Challenge* calls re timechange in afternoon taping.
11:59	Amiel to lunch.

P.M.

12:02	Sun computer system crashes.
12:04	Joan Sutton phones collect from yacht to file a poem for Sunday, entitled *My Love is a Ripe Round Orange*.
12:07	Biodex column cleared.
12:42	Star staffers arrive at Crooks bar to supply latest rumours and trade Trivial Pursuit stock.
12:47	Sun computer system up for two minutes, but has a relapse.
12:52	Winston's quickly seats Barbara Amiel and Paul Godfrey with Star staffers before Star editors arrive to chat up Sun staffers downstairs in the Grill.
12:57	Sun computer system in recovery mode, all copy filed before 12:57 lost forever in mystery bins.
1:10	Morton Shulman arrives with column claiming Scientologists control stock market.
1:12	Sylvia Train photos processed: Al Waxman Eats in New Mexican Restaurant.
1:15	Sara Waxman arrives with Mexican recipes for tomorrow's food page.
1:50	Plain brown envelope arrives for Claire Hoy.
1:55	Male strippers arrive to picket Hoy column.
2:10	Editors consider mid-day possibilities for tomorrow's front photo:

Inflatable Anne Murray Launched
Six Dead in Tractor-Trailer Wheelie
Knowlton Nash Tries Sky-Diving

2:30	Afternoon anti-communist seminar begins with Lubor Zink.
2:48	Paul Godfrey calls for messages. No messages.
3:00	Six SUNshine girls in lobby for promotion photo. Computer system crashes.
3:17	McKenzie Porter column in computer, damning size of ice-cubes in mixed drinks.
3:32	Amiel arrives in office to do tomorrow's editorial. Calls library to get spelling of Konstantin Chernenko.
3:35	Miracle Mart ad pages arrive amid general celebration.
3:45	Paper bumped to 104 pages thanks to Metro-wide tape deck clearance sale.
4:12	Computer system crashes. Hi & Lois comic strip lost.
4:17	First Pizza Pizza delivery of the day.
4:25	Final edition of the Star arrives for use as napkins and coasters under pizzas.
4:30	Videocassette player clearance sale bumps paper to 240 pages.
4:45	Anti-communist seminar for reporters hired since 3:00 p.m.
4:50	SUNshine girl shot for tomorrow available on desk, work stops for 10 minute break.
5:00	Additional coloured ink arrives for videocassette clearance supplement.
5:22	Mayor Art Eggleton arrives for photo opportunity. Proclaims Videocassette Clearance Sale Day in Metro.
5:30	Courier brings Amiel's dry cleaning for evening black tie engagement. Leaves by limo.
5:35	Air Canada brings tickets for Amiel's morning flight to Calgary for luncheon speaking engagement.
5:42	United Press Canada moves nuclear explosion in Europe bulletin.
5:50	Dog arrives to be photographed in clown suit as Pet of the Week.
5:58	Dear Abby column cleared.
6:10	Editors evening meeting to consider early possibilities for front spot colour tomorrow:

Suicide Cult Buys CNE
North York Menaced by Giant Weevil
Tidal Wave in Lake Ontario

6:35	Dr. Lamb column cleared.
6:40	Dunford calls library from bar to get spelling of Konstantin Chernenko.
6:45	Sun computer crashes. Ottawa asked to re-file day's work.

7:40	Sun computer system up in time to take racing results from U.S. tracks.
7:50	Second Pizza Pizza delivery of the day.
7:55	First Swiss Chalet delivery of the day.
8:01	First editors from Star and Globe arrive at Press Club.
8:05	Desk calls library for correct spelling of Waxman.
8:15	Your Horoscope cleared.
8:40	Day editors call from Press Club to ask if anything about a nuclear explosion in Europe is on the wires. Summer student dismisses as crank.
9:12	Chinese food arrives.
9:28	Photos of Barbara Amiel at black tie dinner developed.
9:30	Evening anti-communist rally and prayer for divine guidance.
9:32	City desk takes message from woman who claims Elvis speaks to her through TV set. Route to Bono.
10:11	UPC moves bulletin kill for nuclear explosion. Desk asks summer student to find original story. It's in Entertainment with a photo of Sophia Loren.
10:15	Evening editor's conference for final decision on tomorrow's front:

Santa Slain in Parade Melee
Taco Tragedy Claims Waxman
Sunshine Girl Finds Clothes

10:22	Amiel calls to have editorial read to her.
10:24	Spelling of Konstantin Chernenko corrected in editorial.
10:30	Triple murder in Scarborough.
10:31	Jumbo jet crashes at Malton.
10:32	Computer system crashes after the final race at Greenwood.
10:45	Final art arrives for tape deck supplement.
11:40	Emergency call for additional ink for supplement.
11:55	Photos arrive of triple murder and air crash. Front page re-made, bumping Slain Santa to 42.
12:15	Computer system crashes.
1:00	Bars Close.
1:12	Papers roll.
1:15	First Suns depart by truck for Ottawa.
1:30	Moon comes up over Sun parking lot.

Take the Eh Train

Brian Shein

One evening along about nine o'clock I am sitting in Joe Allen's restaurant on West Forty-Sixth Street putting on a plate of sirloin when the feeling comes to me that something is not right about the place. This restaurant is a very high-class spot and I am fond of it because of the way nothing about it changes, which in the Broadway district is not a matter to be taken lightly. This evening, however, I am suddenly feeling that something about Joe Allen's is changed, and it is making me very nervous indeed.

I take many a gander about the place but I see only the familiar sights such as the checkered tablecloths and the hand-chalked menus which remind me of my happy old-time memories. But then I spot what it is; it is such a shock to my system that I stand bolt upright.

"Moose Murders!"

My tone of voice is such that several parties dining nearby give me the eyeball as if I am grogged up something terrible, but I pay them no attention because what I am seeing is enough to make any guy stand up and yell as if he is being slammed in the kisser.

In case you are not familiar with dropping in on Joe Allen's, there is a famous collection of theatrical posters on the wall which are for plays subject to go bust after opening night. It is a way to make you feel no matter how down you are that there are others on Dream Street who are even more down, and probably deserving it more, too. And if a guy is in Joe Allen's with a doll on a night when there is a big moon over the Hudson, the posters can be a dead cold set-up for them to have some laughs, and him to give her the general idea he is wise to a thing or two. The worst of all these plays that go bust is one called *Moose Murders*, which is one that ought to close before it opens, but I am fond of its poster, which is always there on the wall with a set of antlers and all. But now I see the *Moose Murders* showbill is gone; so are the others. The posters now on the wall are all for hit shows. It makes the hair stand up on the back of my neck.

I try to think of what is going on, and I suspect perhaps with the unemployment situation and banks about to go bust, it is because Joe Allen's is under new management. Or maybe it is something to do with the new Trump Tower which is a big cause of a lot that is wrong with this man's town. I decide to pay the tab and take a fast walk over to Mindy's to look for Judge Goldfobber (who is not a judge but is a sure-footed operator in beating a tough beef), to canvass his opinion in the matter.

Well, no sooner am I out the door when I see this is not Forty-Sixth Street at all. I am standing on the edge of a big, dark parking lot, and I am outside what looks to be a big warehouse, and there are some more warehouses along the street. There is nobody else around, which is not something you see every night in the Broadway district, and the street is wider than it used to be. It is also cleaner. There is no trash anywhere, which is enough to make any guy feel like he is seeing a ghost. Chills run up and down my back. I do not know where I am. I could be in Jersey or worse.

I consider stepping back into Joe Allen's for a quick sample of the liquid merchandise but after the way they misplaced *Moose Murders* I cannot see any percentage in this and will lay plenty of 6 to 5 that stepping back inside is a bigger mistake than what I am doing by standing in a street I have never seen before in my life.

Just then a car pulls up and a guy gets out with a doll. I give them a huge hello and ask where I am. The doll has a little turned-up snozzle and she gives me a mean look like I am just here from Mudville. "SoHo," she says, and they are both in the restaurant before I have a chance to warn them about *Moose Murders*.

I am not sure I want to warn them anyway because when she says "SoHo" it throws me for a loop. I cannot figure out how SoHo jumps this far uptown without a considerable dislocation of the pavement, unless maybe while I am inside some guys from Brooklyn snatch Joe Allen's and dump it down on Spring Street.

I walk until I get to a sign which says "Queen Street." Maybe it means to say Queens, but this is the first time I hear of a borough becoming a street and anyways, how can either of them be SoHo, which is a district and is this side of the East River the last time I looked. Then I hear a sound like ker-thump, ker-thump. I know this is the subway and I feel much improved as I take the stairs down. I know at least I am still in New York because I spot a crowd of the kids who call themselves the Guardian Angels. They are always protecting citizens in the subway which, since I am a law-abiding guy, I thoroughly approve of.

Suddenly they bunch up tight and charge forward down the stairs, so I know they are about to interfere with a mugger. But all I can see they are chasing is a candy-wrapper which is blowing along the platform. Two of the kids run in front of it to block it and two more keep it boxed in from either side while another makes a big somersault in the air, catches the wrapper on the tip of his toe and kicks it high enough that the others grab it and wrestle it to the ground, where it gives up and stops moving. Then they hustle it to a trash can and dump it in without even giving it a chance in front of a judge. That is how the Guardian Angels operate, but since it is only a candy wrapper and the subway platform is as clean as the streets, I get the same bad feeling; goose bumps come out along my arms.

Just then I see a little guy in an overcoat on the platform. I figure him for a newspaper scribe and decide to tell him my story since maybe, if these guys from Brooklyn are turning the city upside down and the Guardian Angels are chasing candy wrappers, there is a fifty-point front page headline in this. Right then the train pulls in and I am lucky to catch hold of his elbow just as the doors are closing. I notice just before I step in that the train is as clean as the platform, without so much as a whisper of spray paint. I am not sure I feel good about stepping into a train like that of my own free will.

It takes me a while to catch the guy's attention since everytime I jog his elbow or bend his overcoat lapels he has a habit of looking away as if I am not there. When I ask which way the train is heading he gives me the same look as the doll with the turned-up snozzle, like I am from the boondocks, and he says, "Uptown."

I get the bright idea to play along, so I tell him I am new in town and ask him to give me the grand tour. He gets friendlier then and allows that he is a newspaper scribe just like I figure him for, and agrees to take me around.

The next thing I know we are out on what he calls Times Square. There is a little billboard which lights up to show the time and the temperature, but the temperature is in what the scribe calls centigrade, which sounds like an insect to me and not any way to tell the temperature. There are some arcades and stores where they sell girlie books but that is all. I think that if I tell Bookie Bob and Dave the Dude that this is Times Square they will say I am subject to fits and lock me in Bellevue for sure.

Then the scribe takes me to a store where it is full of citizens all buying the *The New York Times* and the *Post* and the *Village Voice* and the *New Yorker* and *New York*. I feel more at home here until I ask the scribe which paper he writes for; he tells me that it is none of these so I begin to figure him for a grifter.

He asks me if I want to see the Lower East Side and we ride the subway for what seems long enough to carry a guy to Erie, Penn. and back, and then we get out and look at some nice shops near what he says are the beaches. This is the only time I hear of a beach on the East River, and I hope to God I never live to look at such a thing. So we get back on the subway and he is going on in a loud voice about how the city has grown up and has everything other cities have. We walk along a street which he tells me is just like Fifth Avenue, and I wonder why anyone wants a street just like Fifth Avenue when all he has to do is walk along the real thing. Besides, I see no sign of St. Pat's Cathedral.

The scribe is all excited now, bragging about things as if to make a guy from the boondocks feel about as high as his shoelaces, and then he stops and pulls himself up tall and says, "And of course, I just got back from New York."

That stops me dead in my tracks.

"If you just got back from New York," I says, "then what have we been doing all this time, going crosstown and uptown and over to the East Side and the West Side, and Chinatown and Little Italy and almost Fifth Avenue? From the way you and everyone I meet talks, this *is* New York. So where are we now?"

"Toronto," he says.

"Toronto, Ohio?" I say.

"Toronto, the city," he says. "In Canada."

I get the terrible feeling that maybe this guy and the citizens in the magazine store and the doll at the restaurant are all ghosts. But he shakes my hand goodbye, and it is about as real as shaking hands with Judge Goldfobber, who is not a judge.

The scribe gives an embarrassed little smile and then he turns a corner and is gone.

I look around me. I get the idea now, I think. Toronto is a part of New York that is way uptown past Harlem, maybe five hundred miles uptown, which is why it looks as bit different and is scrambled up, but it is still New York. This makes me feel better so I go back down into the subway to look for the train to take me back down to Forty-Second Street. I am in need of a plate of cold borscht at Mindy's.

Hollywood North

So You Want to Be in Movies...
Learn to Mogul

Ron Base

Introductory Notes: You Too Can Be In The Movie Business.

Of course you want to be in the movie business. Who doesn't? In Toronto being in the movie business is the ultimate glamour. People here are in awe of the movie business, and they are crazy about movies. Why, when movies were an attractive tax deduction (1979-80) Toronto was even known — at least to itself — as Hollywood North!

It should be pointed out that there is not now *anything* that could be called a movie industry in Toronto. But that is beside the point. The fact remains that a great number of people in the vicinity of Bloor Street and Avenue Road, within easy hailing distance of Yorkville Avenue, choose to maintain the fiction — both for themselves and others — that there is an industry and they are part of it.

However, just because no one is making movies, does not mean there are no great opportunities in the Toronto film industry. To the contrary. Because there is no movie industry, there is nothing to stop you getting into it. If people were actually making pictures, they certainly would not be interested in you.

There are, however, a few simple rules that need to be followed, a couple of things you should know before embarking on your Toronto movie career. What follows is applicable only in Toronto. In Hollywood, for example, none of this would work. But then in Hollywood, they occasionally make movies.

Choosing The Right Job

The first thing you must decide is this: what exactly is it that you want to do in the movie industry. You may want to be a film technician of some sort — a cameraman or a cinematographer or a first assistant director — but that would require long periods of apprenticeship and training and let's face it, nobody wants to waste a lot of time.

Likewise, it is probably advisable to stay away from directing, even though it is the most revered job in the movie industry. Here again, some sort of experience is usually required. When you tell people you are a director, they tend to ask about what you have directed. Even if it's only *Kavik, Wild Dog Of The North,* it's something.

Stay away from acting, too. Forget about the Robert Redfords and the Clint Eastwoods, the four or five actors who get paid millions of dollars. The rest, as the late Alfred Hitchcock very correctly pointed out, are cattle. At least they are treated no better than cattle. They live lives of unmitigated hell. Do you really want to spend the next forty years of your life praying for the phone to ring? Besides, actors have neither power nor prestige. You want both.

Some people opt for screenwriting, but you are well advised to stay away from it. If you tell people that you write screenplays, inevitably someone will want to see something that you have written. That could lead to unnecessary embarrassment. If you do write something, it will take an ungodly amount of time, and cause you all sorts of headaches. Screenwriting is no fun. If someone asks to read what you've written, they won't be able to produce it anyway. So what's the use?

No, what you need is something that requires you do absolutely nothing and thus enables you to be somebody. There is only one job in the movie business that allows for that.

The Right Job

Become a movie producer. Producers are the only stars in Canada. Back in the days of the film boom, they hogged all the attention, and they have managed to hang on to it. Maitre d's still give them good tables, local newspapers continue to quote them uncritically, and perhaps most importantly, there are beautiful young actresses and models who readily come with the territory.

What, you may well ask at this point, does a Toronto movie producer do? It's okay. Everyone asks the same question. Don't be concerned. The one thing you will *not* have to do as a movie producer is actually make a movie. There are all sorts of movie producers around who have not made a picture in years, and it hasn't hurt them at all.

In fact, if you are somehow trapped into making a movie, you are in for an absolutely miserable time. It requires that you work long hours, standing around on sets telling arrogant directors they are spending too much time and, worse, too much money. You would have to listen to the gripes of over-the-hill actors who want larger Winnebagos and bigger per diems.

Most Toronto movie producers are content to have lunch and sit around and talk about movies. And hell, even you can do that. Here are the basics that will help you get through the parfait of sweet peppers at the Courtyard Café.

The "Project In Development"

The first thing you must have is a "Project in Development." Every producer has one. This is what you would make if you were actually going to make a movie. When you say, "I have several projects in development at the moment," people tend to nod knowingly.

Soon word will get around: "Fred Smedley, you know, the producer? Yeah, apparently he has several projects in development." This will probably lead at some point to a call from one of the local show business newspaper columnists. Don't get nervous about this. To the contrary. Getting your name in print as a movie producer, confirms that you are indeed a movie producer.

Just be a little careful about what you say for attribution. Show business columnists never check much of anything. They are an amazingly trusting lot, mostly because they are also extremely lazy. However, keep your comments as vague as possible, just to be on the safe side.

For example, if a reporter, or anyone else for that matter, happens to ask you just what projects are in development, use the following reply: "Al, you know there are all sorts of people in this country who go around shooting off their mouths about what they're going to do. I'm not one of those people. When it happens, it happens. You'll be the first to know. All I can say at the moment is that we're close, and I'm very pleased, and very excited."

You will be congratulated for your integrity. Here is a producer who eschews the phony hype. People will begin to look at you with a new respect. You are a no-nonsense sort of guy. A rarity in the movie business. You call a spade a spade. People will want to get to know you. Actors who make a lot of television commercials will leap up from their tables in restaurants and enthusiastically pump your hand. They want you to hire them. Beautiful women and/or men will glance at you appraisingly. They want you to hire them. Everyone wants you to hire them. You are a producer. You are on your way.

Dropping The Right Names

Of course, you cannot go on forever announcing you have "projects in development." Now don't panic. There is nothing to be worried about. This is where that most necessary weapon in the knowledgable producer's arsenal comes into play. The Name Drop.

The Name Drop is simple enough. You merely mention a couple of famous names in connection with your "project in development." Again, keep it vague. Everyone in the movie business has a short attention span. No one would want to hear your details, even if you had them to give.

It should not be necessary to casually say anything more than, "Jane's got the script now, and she loves it, of course." (Use "of course" as much as possible. It lends a reassuring certainty.) Everyone in the movie business is hip. Everyone will automatically conclude that the Jane you mention is Jane Fonda.

If you say, "I was talking to Clint's people last week, they're very excited," no one is going to think the Clint in question is Clint Walker. If they do, you are, to put it mildly, talking to the wrong people.

The Right Names

Now this is important. You may at some point choose to use someone's surname. It is not necessary, but it does lend a certain authority to your conversation. Now, the mistake the novice producer almost always makes is using names that were big when he was actually attending movies regularly. Many of the stars he mentions are now dead. Telling people you have a dead movie star interested in your script, means either you have a hell of a script or you are lying about being a producer.

During the Movie Boom of the late seventies (not a period you should talk about too much, incidentally) producers ran around hiring all sorts of washed-up movie stars because they were the only ones anyone in Toronto had ever heard of. Things have become a trifle more sophisticated since then. Not much, mind you. But somewhat. Herewith is a list of names you should never ever mention in connection with any of your projects:

Rod Steiger	Donald Sutherland	James Coburn
Ernest Borgnine	Kirk Douglas	Orson Welles
Angie Dickinson	Clint Walker	Milton Berle
Richard Harris	Oliver Reed	Donald Pleasance
Robert Mitchum		Sally Kellerman

Useful Words And Phrases

In your new and honourable role as Toronto movie producer you may care to drop the odd knowledgeable word or phrase to reassure the burghers that in talking to you, they are truly on "the inside" of the movie business. What follows can be scattered throughout just about any conversation.

1. "I was talking to Frank Price at Universal the other day, and he says there are only three kinds of movies that the American studios are interested in: comedies, science fiction, and action." Not only does this make you sound as though you have been talking to Frank Price at Universal, but what he says he told you is also true. Be careful about bandying about the names of Hollywood movie executives, though. They change with the same regularity you (hopefully) change underwear.

2. "Sure, you say it's a hit. But what's it doing on a per screen basis?" You don't have to actually know what a picture is doing on a "per screen" basis, except to understand that a picture is usually a hit if it is doing about $4,000 per theatre (or per screen). If it is pulling only $2,000, you can be pretty sure it's a stiff. But no one's going to get you into that kind of detail. Just shout "per screen" a couple of times.

3. "This baby's got legs." You may want to say that about the model coming towards your table. More often, and less chauvinistically, this phrase is used to describe how well a given movie is doing at the box office. If a picture has "legs" then it is holding up nicely. *Flashdance,* for instance, had legs. On and off the screen. *Harry And Son* didn't even have a weekend. Let alone legs.

4. "I appreciate you letting me see this, but I'm afraid it just doesn't fit in with our needs at the moment." To be used if a screenwriter actually gives you a screenplay. Scripts are boring, and hard to read. They give you headaches. As a producer there is no reason to subject yourself to that kind of punishment.

5. "Tell me, my dear. Have you ever considered a career in movies?" Sure it's old and it's hackneyed, but it still works. Remember, you are a producer, so the last thing anyone expects is original dialogue.

Where (And Where Not) To Be Seen

This is probably the most important lesson contained in our primer. Everything you have so far learned is for naught, if you walk into a Macdonald's in Scarborough, and start telling people you are a movie producer. Nobody in Canada has ever seen a Canadian movie, let alone a Canadian movie producer.

With this in mind, it is imperative that you stay within the mid-town Toronto quadrangle formed by Yonge, Bloor, Avenue Road, and Yorkville. In this Gucci-shoed, Givenchy-clad state of unreality, you will be revered. Outside it, you will be ignored. Movie people know this, and seldom leave the safety of the neighbourhood.

The best place to be properly seen, despite a lot of sneering about it, remains the Courtyard Café. Make sure you order a glass of white wine, and the chicken salad at lunch, and whatever happens, don't let them throw you downstairs in the restaurant's pit. This is for the rubberneckers and the tourists. You prefer one of the banquettes at the front, even though they are not particularly comfortable.

The Twenty-Two bar next door to the Courtyard in The Windsor Arms Hotel, has fallen somewhat into disrepute. They remodelled the place recently, and put some tables out along the cobblestones on St. Thomas Street. Even so, it appears to have lost some of its glamour after the heady movie days in the late seventies. Be careful about being seen in there too much. You will not be seen by the right people, anyway.

Noodles, the restaurant on Avenue Road, is still permissible for lunch. But much more au courant among movie folk these days is Il Posto on Yorkville Avenue. The Bellair Café on Bellair Avenue is very popular in summer, if you're in a cruising mood.

Conclusions

That's it. You are now a full-fledged Toronto movie producer. There is one last pitfall to bring to your attention. You will soon feel the urge to make a movie coming over you. Beware! This is a terrible mistake! The movie industry has been plagued by producers who know nothing about movies insisting on making movies. If you decide that you do want to make a movie, then you have failed as a Toronto movie mogul. Find another line of work.

AN MORIRI
AN SUPERESSE MELIOR
IN TORONTO ESSE

RIGHT ORDER OF TORONTO

New to the Queen City? Lost? Lonely?

Drifting in a sea of sophistication and unsure how to cope?
Well, **R.O.T.** can help!
We understand just how daunting Canada's most glamorous city
can be when you're fresh in from Flin Flon.

What Is R.O.T.?

The Right Order of Toronto, a select order of the well-groomed,
is dedicated to the assimilation of newcomers.
We want you to be just like us: happy, healthy, and morally certain
that Toronto is better in every way.

What R.O.T. Can Do For You

• Under the guidance of the Ontario Censor Board we'll teach you the INs and OUTs of correct behaviour and techniques for avoiding person-to-person contact. Including Glance Avoidance, Basic Condescension, Scathing Insults and Spontaneity: How to Avoid It.

• We'll rent you friends for all occasions - brunches, parties, Amway meetings, funerals.

• Provide a great real-estate agent who will guide you past Toronto's enchanting ethnic mosaic on your way to that cute little split-level in Scarborough.

• We'll provide you with the official R.O.T. shopping list; your key to getting the best deals in town from brown shoelaces to bagpipes.

• Your fee includes membership in our vacation paradise CLUB R.O.T. Locations include Gorgeous Grimsby and the tropical Don Valley.

• We'll teach you how to speak like us. Learn to discriminate between lasting issues and passing fads (feminism, nuclear war). Required reading includes: *The Toronto Sun, Reader's Digest* and selected brochures from the Libertarian Party of Canada.

R.O.T. PROVIDES 24-HOUR EMERGENCY SERVICE!

Is R.O.T. For You?

You bet. We have programs for everyone. If your income is over $50,000 per
year, we offer a broad range of lifestyle advice.
(Anyone earning under that amount will be escorted to the airport
and put on the next plane home.)

How Do I Join?

Easy. If you are planning a move to Toronto, give us a call.
R.O.T. representatives will meet you at the airport.

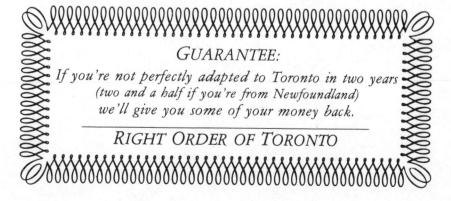

GUARANTEE:

*If you're not perfectly adapted to Toronto in two years
(two and a half if you're from Newfoundland)
we'll give you some of your money back.*

RIGHT ORDER OF TORONTO

Remember The R.O.T. Motto:

DEAD OR ALIVE IT'S BETTER IN TORONTO!

Out and About the Suburbs
Ed Hailwood

North York

Television personality Al Waxman welcomes shrewd Consumers to the Strike Three Shopping Centre (750 recession-conscious merchants under one cantilevered roof). Roses for the fair sex; balloons for casualties; holiday greetings extended by *Penthouse* near-miss Toni Delmonico.

Snelgrove

Book immediately for the Ubermensch Passion Play and Ice-Fishing Derby, in this, its second sensational year. Warning: scenes of flotation may vex the uninitiated. ("If you have tears, prepare to shed them now." — *The Globe*.)

Brampton

Go "behind the scenes" at the world-renowned Hospital for Sick Businessmen. A pulse-quickening *son-et-lumière* depicts state-of-the-heart hernia and cardiac transplants. All donations gratefully accepted.

The Beaches

What The Butler Saw premieres at the Katz Pyjamas Dinner Theatre. Between performances, the all-nude, non-equity cast presents table dancing and flash-frozen Margaritas. Indefinite run.

Buttonville

Creationalist Field Day. Anti-evolution forces gather at Snood's Tavern, site of an abortive 1831 uprising-on-demand. Questionable paperbacks consigned to the compost heap; prominent authors burned *in absentia*. Dress warmly.

Gormley

Soft-Tech Open. Selected malls play host to brain-damaged electronic gamesters. Glue-sniffing grand finale caps two days of hard-fought hand-eye co-ordination. Tatoos for the winners; service industry "management trainee" positions for runners-up.

Stouffville

(Weather permitting) Unveiling of the Garden Gnomes. Priceless ceramic heirlooms come out of the closet. Not recommended for children under the age of discrimination.

Bramalea

Commuters in Motion. A Metro-wide delight. Thousands of shuttle-bugs, customary patrons of the GO Transit network, take their cars and creep along congested access routes, singing traditional melodies ("I am driving in from Bramalea / I never see / My family / Is there any place you'd rather be? / It's Bramalea for me!" — to the tune of *Marching to Pretoria*). Pitch your tent early to ensure an unimpeded peek.

Willowdale

The Seventh-Largest Lawn Sale east of Winnipeg. Even-numbered houses, Yetta Sluiceway, noon till nine. Astounding bargains in fondue sets, personal computers and first-born male children. Small sandwiches only.

Mimico

Pre-Owned Vehicles of the Golden Triangle. Skilled craftspersons blend sawdust and transmission oil, fine-tune odometers and consult with their counterparts from Quebec on the availability of hard-to-locate spare parts. No money down.

South Pickering

Door-Crasher Opening of Miniature Metro, located a scant 15 kilometres north of the bustling 401. Gasp at a six-inch-high CN Tower; thrill to the barely visible NDP schoolboard trustee; admire the tiny, perfect features of a seventy-two-year-old street hustler. Guaranteed to put "big-city" problems in perspective!

Downsview

Disavowel of Alien Influences. Borough mayor offers sacrifices, in vain attempt to ward off an influx of loose-living trendies, jovial pimps and militant feminists. Divination by entrails follows in many areas; consult local listings. Folk dancing permitted.

Etobicoke

Roadside Attraction Round-Up. All Northbound routes. Canny entrepreneurs capture the attention of passing cottage-goers, with cunningly placed strands of piano wire. Don't forget to duck.

Ajax

To Survey With Love. As a long, hot summer unfolds, next-door neighbours of long standing square off over boundary disputes dating back to 1968. To the victors go the lot lines!

Islington

Two Hundred Years of Bowling Costume at a Glance. Larger-than-life replicas, cast in never-fade cellulite, bring lumps to every thorax. See also the John Turner Butter Sculpture (admission 50 cents).

Agincourt

Rally. Gay Single Parents Against Everything. The Jane-Finch Corridor springs to richly textured diversity, as cheering watchers hurl shredded welfare cheque stubs from high-rise balconies, creating their own "ticker-tape parade." ("A sad indictment of outmoded planning procedures." — *The Star*. "We told you so." — *The Sun*.)

Scarborough
October 31st — Midnight.

All-Condos Eve. Rental properties miraculously converted at dead of night. Celebrate the expulsion of fixed-income pensioners.

Don Mills

Ribbon-cutting marks the opening of a seventy-two storey "kiss-and-make-up" parking garage, adjacent to TTC, LCBO and PCB disposal site. Crowning of "Miss Graffiti," Toni Delmonico. Don't forget your spray can.

Hagerman's Corners

Unusual Lingerie at 5 Bideawee Crescent. Knock twice and ask for "Marlene." Television personality Al Waxman offers franchises for those who dare to be great.

Todmorden

Super Showcase of "Arms-Length" Origami, the graceful art of bureaucratic paper-shuffling, worth a memorable visit. Digital watches ($69.95) for accompanied youngsters facilitates precise count-down of shopping days remaining until Christmas.

Locust Hill

Adoration of the Developers. "Three Wise Builders" bring precious gifts to chosen aldermen, in hushed candlelit ceremonies at selected all-nite milkstores.

Numerous Venues

Changing of the Traffic Lights. Call Ontario tourist office for details.

Coming Soon

Raising of the Mill Rate. Behind closed doors in widely scattered civic offices. Times and places to be announced, or not, depending.

The Agony of Victory
The Thrill of Defeat

Alison Gordon

True Torontonians begin each day with a silent prayer. Before their sit-ups and deep-breathing exercises, before they have even begun to contemplate their granola, they thank the deity of their choice for Harold Ballard. Single-handedly, Ballard has kept Toronto's most important sports tradition alive. Pal Hal and the Maple Leafs he owns are the last of the great Toronto losers.

As long as Ballard continues to meddle with the hockey team, as long as he keeps bad-mouthing his players and playing George Steinbrenner North, Torontonians can still hang their heads and consider themselves truly second-rate. They can contemplate their own personal scalawag, as mean-spirited a character as can be found in all of sport, and smile. (Outsiders may not recognize a Torontonian's smile. It consists of a quick, almost undetectable grimace at the lips, similar to the rictus caused by a serious gas attack among the citizens of any other metropolis.)

These past few years have been confusing for sports fans, settled as they were in the security of unrelieved mediocrity. In the good old days, death, taxes, and sports teams that choked were the constants of Toronto life. Sportswriters had to write about the Argos' and Maple Leafs'

Grey and Stanley Cup chances before the first game of each season, because the teams would never be so close to the top again. The Blue Jays and the Blizzard came to town and fit right in. But in 1981, the dreadful changes began.

First, over the protests of politicians worried about being vomited upon, permission was given to sell beer at baseball and football games. The Blue Jays and Argos began to win. (The Gardens, incidentally, are still dry.) In 1982, the Blue Jays crawled out of the cellar and the Argos went all the way to the Grey Cup. That they lost it that year at home was only a tribute to the gloomy influence of the Toronto fans.

That loss came just in the nick of time. Still, there were ten wins that year. And a tie. The fans began to understand that their teams couldn't be counted on to blow it every time. It has led to a mass identity crisis.

In the old days, it was easy. There was no need to worry about the behaviour at the stadium. The preferred Torontonian response, cordial silence, was completely appropriate to what was transpiring on the field of play. Even the rambunctious held themselves in check until the seventh inning stretch, when civil servants in track suits grimly led the crowd in exercises.

But winning demands more: cheering, standing ovations, hoarse cries of encouragement. It started slowly, in pockets around the stadium. A tentative "Let's go, Blue Jays!" hurled into the silence as people for a dozen rows around stared in disbelief. There was more. When the animated clapping hands appeared on the scoreboard, oh, at least several joined in. When the taped bugle charge sounded, you could actually hear brave souls yelling "charge!"

By 1983, it was so crowded and noisy at games it was impossible to doze off, and by the time Grey Cup rolled around a new breed of Torontonian had evolved: the Winning Sports Fan.

There he was, on the front page of the *Toronto Sun* the day after the Argos took Lord Grey's battered mug. He was in his early twenties, standing on the hood of a car on Yonge Street in the cold, expressing his joy, no, the joy of a whole city. He had drunk himself stupid and taken all his clothes off in the awe of the moment. I bet his Mum was proud.

Winning sports fans are now everywhere, as much a part of Toronto as Casa Loma, and just as derivative. They have learned their behaviour from television. They wear revolting oversized foam rubber hands with the index finger pointing skyward and shout "We're Number One!" just like they do at Redskins games. They paint their faces blue. When an official makes a call against the home team, they chant "Bullshit, bullshit," just like they do in Yankee Stadium. They have even caught on to "Na na na na, na na na na, hey hey-ey goodbye!" just like the guys at the Montreal Forum, who stole it from Comiskey Park. They even discovered The Wave, via Detroit, via Oakland, via Michigan State University.

Up to date? You'd better believe it! Hey, Torontonians finally know how to have fun. Just look at baseball's opening day. They showed up in the thousands and did it in style. They got drunk, brawled in the line-ups in the men's rooms, pissed in the sink and threw up in the ramps. They left before the game was over because the beer taps were turned off. But not before one of their number streaked the stadium, leaving his undies in centre field.

You don't even have to see the new breed to recognize them. Their distinctive cry of "ARRRR-goooos" gives them away every time. They bray it at football games, baseball games, cricket matches and lawn bowling finals.

The cry echoes in subway stations, in line at movies, at rock concerts, high school graduation ceremonies, weddings, bar mitzvahs and Liberal nomination meetings.

Toronto politicians, no dummies, realize that this group is made up of political virgins whose collective energy is as yet untapped. Correctly assessing their mean intelligence, the politicians are offering them a dome. A dome! A dream come true if you don't like sport. A haven for the guys who treat the ballpark as a great big tavern. They can take their clothes off without worrying about wind and rain. They can shout obscenities and listen to them echo around the arena. And with a brand new titty dome next to the phallic CN tower, how can Toronto not become the envy of the civilized world?

As for the prune-faced purists who can't stand seeing other people have fun, never fear. They still have a refuge. You can find them all winter long, sitting sedately in the golds at the Gardens. Those unfortunates who don't like hockey, and the football and baseball fans who crave mediocrity, they have only one alternative. They have to move to Montreal.

Not the National Capital

The Politics of Dull, Boring and Ineffectual

Michael Enright

If Toronto politics were a food, it would be a nice rice pudding, with a few raisins scattered in. Or perhaps a meat loaf, hold the *HP*. No condiments, no pepperoni, no spicy stuff. Toronto, politically, is the bland God gave to Cain. In Toronto politics, bland is beautiful and the people and the politicians love it that way.

Prior to becoming mayor, Arthur Eggleton, the Gomer Pyle of municipal politicians, was a cost accountant. He had pursued that career because his parents had told him that selling life insurance was too racy a life for a Toronto boy. No one in town can spell his name or remember anything he has ever said or done, except that he was the guy who beat John Sewell for the job. (Sewell is remembered as the guy who used to wear leather jackets to City Council meetings.)

Eggleton is, however, a very nice man. And while being mayor of the city is a nice job, it does not come with a lot of what they call "clout."

Toronto is really part of a larger enclave called Metropolitan Toronto or Metro in the low argot of the *Toronto Star*. Two people run Metro. One is the Metro Chairman. For years this was a powerful suburban politician named Paul Godfrey. He was world famous in Toronto for two reasons: bringing professional baseball to the city and for having a lot of his chin removed so he wouldn't have to pay extra fare for it on the subway.

The second person who runs Metro Toronto and indeed the Metro Chairman is William Davis, the Premier of all the Ontarios. Billy, as no one calls him to his face, comes from Brampton, a smallish Toronto ex-urb whose main industries are ladies who take off all of their clothes and a coin-operated car wash. Billy Davis is a Tory, and the Tories have ruled Ontario for more than forty years. Therefore they and he have clout (which is why the Metro Chairman never calls Billy Davis "Billy" to his face).

Most of the power on Metro Council, the overall body of governance of the area, is held by representatives of the suburbs: Scarborough, Etobicoke, York, East York and North York. There is, alas, no York York. Since more people live in the suburbs than live in the city, suburban politicians, outnumbering their city colleagues as they do, can make life a living hell for Toronto folk.

The suburban mayors are very sensitive. For instance, they didn't like it when their areas were called "townships," so they became "boroughs." The mayors are also very turf-sensitive, particularly about the fact that their areas look like the moon on a rainy Tuesday afternoon.

North York, for instance, run by a former refrigerator salesman, makes Sudbury look like Juan-les-Pins.

People are not allowed to live in the suburbs of Toronto unless they own a car and belong to the Rotary Club. They must also curl in the winter and barbecue in the summer. For fun, the average Etobicoke family drives to the airport to watch the planes refuel. In Scarborough, the big local event is the annual Muffler Repairman of the Year Olympics. East York, which is more sedate and contains the British outpost of Leaside, wants to print its own money and re-fight the Boer War.

Years ago, city people thought it would be nice to live in the suburbs. The open spaces, the under-crowded schools, the great little shopping centres, all proved to be a powerful magnet to the burgeoning middle class; the exodus began. But after a time the magic wore off. Parents suddenly found their children bringing home hub caps after school. Crabgrass took on the importance of Swine Flu. A Sunday dinner out meant dragging the family to the neighbourhood Whoopsyburger down at the plaza. The novelty of a cultural evening at the Bowlaway soon dissipated. People began to think there was more to urban life than miniature golf. So the exodus went into reverse and people began to move back into the city. The suburban sachems were not at all pleased and formed a political bloc to vote against any progressive measure initiated by city politicians. The war has continued over many years and many issues.

The greatest bone of contention on Metro Council is what to do with the Islanders. Some two hundred and fifty doughty settlers live in small cottages on the Toronto Islands. The women all wear snoods and make their own candles, while the menfolk go to sea every morning by taking the ferry to Bay Street. The suburbanites would like them removed and their houses bulldozed in order to make way for a parking lot. Or a Pershing missile launch pad. The city politicians feel the quaint Islanders add a touch of pioneer colour in the vast pen-and-ink landscape.

The other major issues facing Toronto may not seem, at first blush, likely to incite riotous response. But they are as visceral as Toronto issues ever get.

Dog poop, for instance. There are fifty thousand dogs in the city and they all have to go somewhere. A bylaw was passed limiting leashed dogs to specifically designated poop parks, so sparing the majority of bosky acreage for people. The fine for unlawful doo-doo is $1,000.

The issue split the city in two. The rhetoric between the lovers of the dog and the lovers of the park resonated with angry words and shaking fists. Corrugated old men collapsed over the hairy flanks of aging Labradors. Squeaky women shook their Lhasa apsos in high rage. The park lovers threatened to nail 96 feces to the door of City Hall. It was a terrible time, but it was settled without the spilling of blood.

The other big issue is whether to build a domed stadium to replace the worst baseball park in the universe, Exhibition Stadium. And if to have one, where to put it. The suburban loonies want it on their turf. After much study and money, a blue-ribbon panel (established by Premier Davis), suggested a spot in Downsview. Unfortunately this was right at the end of a runway for armed forces planes and would have meant paving the outfield with foam for incoming jets.

Premier Davis, a baseball fan himself, opts for an indoor playing field where he can be warm when he's not in Florida watching baseball out-of-doors. The purists want the game played the way Jesus played it, on God's real grass, complete with rain delays. When Toronto finally does get its dome, it will thrust the city into the ranks of such world-class cities as Indianapolis and Seattle.

The last major issue in Toronto is the question of expressways and, here again, Premier Billy plays the benign role of the old compromiser. Torontonians are obsessed by and about expressways. The suburbanites want plenty more of them so they can drive everywhere. The city dwellers want none of it; they loathe expressways. Whichever position is held, most people and most politicians are thinking about expressways at least twice a day.

Since downtown parking is becoming more expensive than housing, the city politicians are trying to keep cars out of the city. But because most cars live in the suburbs and work in the city, exurbanites scream for more highways. It will be left to Der Preem to settle the matter with a smile, a puff of pipe-smoke and a completely unintelligible policy statement.

Which is the way Torontonians really want it. Politics in Toronto is a kind of indoor sport — with winners and losers and scorecards. Even if politics really mattered (as some say it does in Montreal and Edmonton), it's doubtful that the citizenry would rise above the politics of the dull, the boring and the ineffectual.

Contention makes Toronto nervous. Decision-making is dangerous because there is a chance the wrong one will be made. Better to lie low and argue about doggie doo-doo and trenchant Islanders.

After all, what's so bad about being a big Grimsby?

THE VIEW FROM AWAY

Somewhere out there, beyond the Don and the Humber and
Terminal 2, lies the rest of the country: making notes, keeping
lists, trying to understand us.

They really don't like Toronto. Those that say they do are the
ones that think they may have to move here some day, so they
try not to offend.

But it's a known fact that in the time it has taken you to read
this, 132 Canadians have made snide remarks about
"Hogtown."

Is it our sophistication? Our easy grace with fame, money and
richly-deserved success? Is it Knowlton Nash with his rakish
good looks and devil-may-care outlook on the problems
of the nation?

What is it about us that irks them so?

Memo To: Toronto
From: The Rock

Ray Guy

When you try to come to grips with Toronto, sex is what you run head and ears into.

This comes as a nasty fright to those still working with the city's reputation of twenty years ago. Then, the only evidence at all of such a thing rested with the livestock exhibits at the CNE. There was a rumour of a couple living in sin on Spadina Avenue but they, of course, had come from Sardinia.

It's the sociologists who've done it. Taking their cue from chicken hatcheries, they've discovered that cities can be sexed. Hence we have the First Principle that while Montreal is female, Toronto is male.

To the layman, this is not readily apparent. If you squint at a map of the Montreal islands in a poor light, yes, there may be something about the shape that might possibly bring a blush to the convent-reared cheek. Chuck in that city's bosomy basilicas, its sensuous domes, the pervasive scent of Papist incense in the air, the ladies undergarments in the shop windows (the cut of which you would never have seen in Eaton's catalogues until lately), and, yes, some sort of a case might be made.

With Toronto, it's not so easy. Turn a map of the area every which way and, even with a prurience verging on the deranged, there's not a helluva a lot you can divine from it. It's on a peninsula, to be sure, but nothing can be made of the shape of that, even with reference to those cautionary sex hygiene films used by the military.

There are all those thrusting office towers but sometimes — as Freud might have told us — an office tower is nothing more nor less than a support system for coffee machines. When it was first raised, the CN tower was leapt upon by those eager to copperfasten the theory. Alas, no dice. That slim, gigantic shaft soaring up from the former stockyards prompted a few brave souls to recall Paul Bunyan's blue ox, Babe.

But Babe was, of course, a female and even her brother, Gabe, was surgically disqualified. Anyhow, all this would have done was take us right back to the livestock exhibits at the CNE and that is no progress at all.

In truth, Toronto may be inclining more and more toward the "Middle Way" as your ancient Greeks would have it, . . . or "pansyfication," as your Uncle Alf would have it.

The popular press has stressed the growing contingent of the light-of-foot on Toronto's streets. This is, perhaps, unfair. Here, as in any other great city, it is normal that "gays" make up a good portion of the woof, not to mention the warp. Perhaps it is the aggressive vociferousness of the "gay community" in Toronto that thrusts it so much to the forefront of the national consciousness. The peccadillo that once dared not speak its name cannot now, for love nor money, be persuaded to stick a cork in it.

Your correspondent lately sat, one Sabbath morning in early May, in a downtown hotel room switching back and forth, for the novelty of it, among Portuguese, Islamic, Germanic, Presbyterian and Gerry-Falwellian TV preachers, who were all railing against the sinful lusts of the world, the flesh and the devil. The balconies of the thirty-storey slab of an apartment building opposite gradually filled with duos and trios of chaps bearing coffee mugs, their gold chains, medallions and earrings glinting in the early sunlight.

Now and then they would wave pleasantly in the direction of the hotel. I wondered what the protocol might be and turned up the volume of God's TV messengers. As it transpired, the lads were merely waving at each others' reflections in a mirror-glassed office tower behind the hotel.

However, the essence of Toronto still seems to be the arrow-straight WASP. Granted, it seems vaguely indecent to think of Toronto's WASP heart and of sex at the same time. There's an odd compulsion to use the old euphemism "It." The notion of "Them" actually doing "It" is like trying to picture Bill Davis doing the moonwalk.

But as the flood of "ethnics" has risen in recent years, our WASP has discovered the pleasures of the flesh, or at least two of them; food and exercise. He, his briefcase, his wife, his office building, and his smile have grown thinner now that he has learned the joys of squash, sweat, steam and sushi.

The only cold comfort left to the ragged but happy peasantry of a place like Newfoundland is the self-lacerating streak of Calvinism in old Toronto. They don't really enjoy themselves, we convince ourselves. By God, if we carefree Catholics — both Roman and Anglican varieties — ever got our hooks into all that, we'd gambol in the hot tubs, wallow in the fettucine Natasha, and gorge on corn-fed beef with nary a twinge of guilt!

Devine Qui Vient Souper?
(Guess Who's Coming to Dinner?)

Serge Grenier

In 1956 I knew this about Toronto: it was the second-largest city in Canada; it had the first subway system in the country; it was where my great-uncle Donat's secret love (her name was Juliette) had her own TV show; and its inhabitants called their home town Hogtown or The Queen City. I didn't know why. Toronto was to me, and to most other French-Canadians, a remote and severe Protestant city all wrapped up in the British flag.

By 1978 I was living there — to my great surprise. I had an apartment in Rosedale. I didn't know how big a deal this was until I met a fellow Montrealer in a bar. He asked where I lived, I told him. "Pretty good for a French-Canadian," he pouted. He, an anglo who'd come west looking for a better job (i.e., one where he didn't have to speak French), was stuck in a bachelorette on Spadina. In his mind anglos lived among trees and brick mansions, and francos amid tenements and garment factories.

He was not the only English-Canadian I confused. My landlord in Toronto was a relatively young business executive. A bachelor. A swinger. His dinner parties drew the most beautiful women in the city. One day he invited me to a seven-to-midnight dinner party. (I've always been puzzled by this habit of specifying at what time you want your guests to leave.) I was introduced to everybody. "Serge," said one of the guests, "that's Russian, isn't it? Like the famous film-maker Sergei Eisenstein?" "No," corrected a sensuous blonde who looked very much like Juliette to me, "it's Brazilian. Don't you know Sergio Mendes?" I was to learn much later in the evening that she knew more about the bossa nova than she did about films from the USSR.

This confusion about my name was perpetual in Toronto. I very quickly learned to say my name, then spell it. If I had been born Walenti Wojciechowski or Toos Vanheerswynghels, I wouldn't have been surprised by this constant spelling, but Serge Grenier is so easy.

The guests at this dinner party were intensely curious.
"Where did you learn to speak English?"
"Oh, you're a writer. What do you write?"
"Why did you leave Montreal?"
"Are you a separatist?"
"Do you like Toronto?"
"You don't look like a French Canadian!"
I was wearing an Oxford grey suit and Gucci shoes. What did they expect, a white belt?
"Do you speak Parisian French or Québec French?"(That question was posed in Canajan, not British English.)
At 11:50 the place was jam-packed; ten minutes after midnight it was empty.

I spent eighteen months in Toronto. A pleasant stay, all things considered. I got used to bars that closed too early, quiet days in Rosedale, eggs Benedict at every brunch I was ever invited to, noisy subway cars, the inescapable CN tower and a nauseating jingle that insisted that the best caviar in the world comes from Sturgeon Falls, Ont. Right fish, wrong river.

I once saw Pierre Berton autographing a wall in a Chinese restaurant and I frequently watched Maureen Forrester shop for watercress at the Rosedale supermarket. But as a French writer in Toronto, I wasn't making a whole lot of money — and that's considered slightly suspicious in The City That Works. So I moved my head office back to Montreal . . . where I write about Toronto for the French papers.

Our readers are so curious about Toronto:
"Do they have any decent restaurants yet?"
"Can you get a drink after midnight?"
"Do they still have the Orange parade?"
"Whatever happened to Juliette?"

Pacific Blues

Vicki Gabereau

Hey, I like Toronto. I really do. What does it matter that you can't get a view of the place without flying up the side of some huge building, or that in summer a body is required to remain deadly still in bed or be rendered a grease spot by dawn? Who cares if turning on the tap causes your eyes to water? So what if your glasses snap in two convenient pieces in January while walking door-to-door doing market surveys because a job cannot be found? JOB . . . that is the key to having a fulfilled life in Toronto. I learned the trick to full employment: Lie. Lie on the application form, especially about education, put down anything, any university, any college. Go ahead, inflate your higher learning credentials. Have no fear of being found out, press on undaunted. I'll tell you why.

Toronto employers rarely, if ever, check out-of-province references. I suspect it is the fear of Time Zones. There is, after all, only one real time. British Columbia institutes of higher learning do not reveal any scholastic records without a written request from the candidate. You too, can be a Ph.D. in the subject of your choice in seconds. I have had some truly great jobs in Toronto, using this technique. Do you remember the Yonge Street Mall? No, well some of us remember it too well. They closed Yonge Street from Dundas to Gerrard, for some weeks during the summers of 1972-3. It created havoc with the traffic flow but I made a fortune slinging beer at Le Coq D'Or. A pal wrote to me to ask if I really did have a job at the Cock Door. She was nearly right. Now I'm sure I only got that job because of the Time Zone Phobia Theory. The cab driving job which came next, was clearly the result of a bogus M.A. in something . . . Art History, I think. Art History is a good one and popular too. It is ever so hard to pin down.

Wanna know what is really swell about Toronto? A little or even a lot of baloney is not just forgiven but encouraged . . . revered even. Name a city that has had so many near-lunatics offered as mayoral candidates. The day will come, if it hasn't already, that one of them will be elected and that will really put the place on the map.

Toronto has many a distinction. It is the Donut Capital of the World. You didn't know that? Surely it must be displayed in banner form somewhere, on the front page of at least one prominent paper. You can add them up. There are more donut parlours in the Metro area than there are lawyers. No, I take that back, than there are psychiatrists. Maybe that's not right either, . . . but for certain there are more donut outlets than gas stations and liquor stores open after 7 p.m. I'd never even heard of a cruller before hitting Toronto. Beams are prominent in my family so living in the Donut Capital of the World can be a challenge.

Toronto also holds the singular Canadian distinction of having more restaurants with stupid names than any other . . . Who wants to eat at a place called Rickets? Maybe it's closed now. What is so wrong with calling a restaurant one of the old charming names like La Scala, Winston's or Napoleon. Dandy little eateries with names you can understand . . . There was a place on Carlton that sold soft ice-cream into which was tossed all manner of things; chocolate chips, bits of cantaloupe, anything you wanted . . . I asked for linoleum slivers but they didn't think it was at all funny. It was called Lickets and Crackets. I never liked that name, it made me nervous. It must have had the same effect on other people, because now it sells stickers.

I love Toronto. It's a great place. You can get bagels there, its very close to Montreal, and for a small sum a tour can be taken on the street car twenty-four hours a day. Sounds almost too good to be true, doesn't it? There are drawbacks, however, especially for a western type. I mean, if you're from the east coast, it is possible to find, on any given Saturday night, great clots of Maritimers banded together speaking in a familiar tongue and partying it up as only they can. Transported Newfoundlanders face no problems locating their fellow islanders for social occasions and a plate full of flipper pie. Club after club has been set up to make the Italians, Portuguese or Estonians feel at home. So where is a culturally adrift British Columbian to go to drown her sorrows or to celebrate small victories? Where can she go to have a great slab of white bread dripping with Rogers Golden Syrup? When was the last time a couple of Torontonians got together and had a good long chat about the rain . . . or droned on, long into the night about how it is that the Socreds manage to keep a stranglehold on an otherwise sane province? Perhaps westerners are neglected because we don't talk funny, have no particular accent or way of going? Maybe if we had a truly west coast music, our presence would be felt: "Salmon Songs We All Know and Love," "Bella Coola Blues," "Sing Me A Song Of Boston Bar," stuff like that. A club of our own is what is required. Something woodsy, nothing too chi-chi, realism is what we're after. A big sign hanging over the bar with appropriate "club rules": No Wheeling; No Dealing; No Talking at Mach 2; No Chicken Fingers; No Spritzers; No Cassis. That would cover it. What I don't understand is why no entrepreneurial British Columbian has hopped to it already. (Can you use entrepreneurial and British Columbia in the same sentence?)

A Few Words on the Great
Toronto/Montreal Rivalry

Jon Kalina

Dateline Montreal — ''Canada's Best City''

The great Toronto/Montreal rivalry? Are you kidding? What rivalry? One city's the Paris of the New World — lovely women, great food, and a mountain in the middle; the other is filled with day-trippers wearing checked polyester triple-knit suits — and those are the sophisticates. One city's crippled with debt for its extravagant, crazy ideas, and is run by a mayor who was first elected in the Middle Ages. The other city is very neat and orderly, probably runs its finances in the black, and is very serious about jaywalking. Guess which city is which?

Who can compare these two cities? Montreal is a wonderful town pockmarked with crazy faults. Our city administration makes Moscow's look open. We have a police force that wears enormous moustaches and habitually rides the wrong way up the street on the way to a three-hour lunch. And we've lost most of our trees. We're a nutso multi-lingual city where you have to speak both official languages just to buy a quart of milk.

Toronto, on the other hand, is not crazy. The police all look like Mounties, and they'll throw you in jail for littering. In Toronto you get plenty of rest and exercise. If you speak French you get the same bewildered and hostile stare you'd get if you gave a New York cab driver a Canadian ten-dollar bill. Montrealers love their city despite everything. Torontonians tell you theirs isn't as bad as it used to be.

I know, I know. I'm not being fair. But a Montrealer can't be fair about Toronto. It isn't allowed. But I admit my prejudices. I don't know Toronto. I don't like Toronto. (This is the way I used to feel about turnips.) I don't want to hear that it's better than it used to be. I don't want to hear that the buildings are nice or that it's got some very good restaurants now, and that it always had a better art museum. I don't care. When my friends move there I wish them well and I say goodbye. They always say, "Now you have a place to stay when you come to Toronto." Great. It's like having a place to stay in Irkutsk as far as I'm concerned. If they have to move, why don't they move to Rome or Madrid? I could use friends in those cities.

"But you haven't given the city a chance," say my friends. They're right. In fact I've only been there twice. I've spent more time in Tokyo than in Toronto, and with good reason. Tokyo didn't steal all our head offices. Not that we really want them back. Keep them, and keep the banks, too. And keep all our Anglo refugees. They can't come back anyway because we bought their houses cheap when they left. OK, they can come back, but only if they send their kids to Greek school for two years as penance.

"Toronto is the largest city in Canada." So says Statistics Canada. So what? Ouagadugoo is the largest city in Upper Volta, and I don't want to live there either. Does this sound irrational? Nasty? Facile? Do I have anything substantive to say against Toronto? One salient fact that would clinch my argument? Yes I do. Something worse than the checked pants. Worse than the sterile "renovated" neighbourhoods that have been gentrified to within an inch of their lives. Even worse than Toronto's smug consumerism. It's the DIAGONAL PARKING! Small time! So forget your neat golden buildings and your chic shops along whatever street it is. Forget the high salaries and the corporate board rooms. Diagonal parking puts you in the same league as Burlington, Vermont. You may have a lot of money . . . but you're still Hogtown.

Chastened? Doing a slow burn? Mad as hell and not gonna take this anymore? Alright, here's your chance to talk back. Grab a pen. Check off the snappy comeback that best expresses your deepest feelings about Montreal.

Dear Jon...

Jon Kalina
4626 St. Catherine Street West
Montreal Québec
H3Z 1S3

Dear Jon,

You (□ clever boy □poor misguided fool □miserable chauvinist). Why are you (□rubbing our noses in our shortcomings? □ twisting selected facts out of all proportion? □ flogging this poor dead horse?). We here in Toronto *know* that Montreal is (□ the most glamourous city in the world □ a faded relic □ a morally, economically and politically bankrupt backwater). We know Montrealers are (□ chic, sophisticated and cosmopolitan □ sadly deluded losers □ ignorant assholes). Your (□ perceptiveness □ self-importance □ gall) is absolutely astounding.

As for this so-called rivalry (□ you win □ we've been ahead since November 15th, 1976 □ it only exists in the twisted minds of parochial Montrealers who can't cut it in Toronto). You (□ rightly point out □ exaggerate □ rant hysterically about) Montreal's (□ legendary □ over-rated □ completely phony) sophistication. Expo '67 was (□ Canada's finest hour □ a nice, but awfully expensive party □ a long time ago). Mount Royal (□ is a shining example of Montreal's quality of life □ is still standing only because we invented the idea of green space □ should erupt again as soon as possible). The Olympic Stadium

(□ is a glorious monument to the Olympic ideal □ still isn't paid for, has no roof and might collapse □ is an expensive, gigantic concrete bidet unfit for man, beast or sports).

The quality of life in Montreal (□ sparkles with joie de vivre □ could be improved with some sand-blasting, white paint and asparagus fern □ stinks — especially when the wind blows in off that sewage-infested river). Montreal restaurants (□ are miles better □ have yet to discover pink peppercorns □ can't even serve a decent shrimp cocktail). Cultural life in Montreal (□ features the best of Europe and America □ suffers from a lack of Broadway shows and good American movies □ consists of a third-rate wax museum, nude table-top dancers, and indigestible steamed hot dogs). Your civic politics (□ have style and grandeur □ are sadly undemocratic and parochial □ are a throwback to the Dark Ages).

Your civic leaders (□ stand up for what they believe in □ bend to whatever political wind happens to be blowing □ have snouts and eat at troughs). Following Québec's lead in linguistics, we should (□ embrace French as an official language □ offer one or two bilingual services □ ban French in public places — including restaurants).

But thanks for writing, Jon. If it weren't for Montreal and Montrealers we'd (□ still be a dry, dusty and tight-assed hick town □ have no example of failure to drive us onwards and upwards □ have no one to sneer at but the Newfs.)

Sincerely yours,

Ticket to Toronto Magazine

More Pages INSIDE

The Postlethwaite Papers

INSIDE
AN INTELLIGENCE OPERATION

Operation Tailgate nets
MPP Nigel Grogan, his wife
and Quads (born half-an-hour apart)
on a "suspiciously ordinary" vacation

The Postlethwaite Papers

A reconstruction of one of the most famous undercover operations in Metro Police history "Operation Tailgate"

Carsten Stroud

On June 27, 1984, Metro Toronto Police Special Courier Fenley Postlethwaite, distracted by an interior problem connected with his wife's mania for argyle underwear, stepped off a curb at the intersection of Jarvis and Bloor seven seconds too soon. He promptly ricocheted off the fender of a pastry van and into the pages of history. His government issue K-mart attaché case went spinning across the street. The Top Secret papers in it fluttered to earth at the feet of a passing journalist. Lying in front of him in a litter of Twinkies and Moon Doggies, were the documents that would eventually shake the shrubbery of Tory Ontario right down to its roots.

The Postlethwaite Papers (as they eventually came to be called) contained the details of what amounted to an all-out war on the democratic process, led by a secret band of ultra-wackos in the Intelligence Branch of the Toronto Police Department.

The journalist present at that historic fender-bender was a nearly famous local writer celebrated for his hard-hitting inquiries into such Toronto scandals as the overstarching of shirts at Embassy Cleaners and the cover-up of health problems related to executive-length socks. Sweeping the papers into his oversized Ed's Warehouse shopping bag, he crept furtively off to the Bridal Suite of the Sea Horse Motel on Lakeshore Boulevard, where he locked himself in. Then he went over every aspect of the Postlethwaite Papers with a fine-toothed comb.

This is his reconstruction of one of the most famous undercover operations in Metro Police history.

The most bizarre story to surface in the Postlethwaite Papers began with a secret RCMP communiqué direct to Metro Intelligence Headquarters in the basement of Willard Hall Women's Christian Temperance Union on Gerrard Street. The coded communiqué was a tip that Cuban Terrorist Infiltrators were being landed along the boardwalk in The Beaches.

These Cuban saboteurs were to be co-ordinated by an offical in the Ontario government, a respected party backbencher by the name of Nigel Grogan. According to the RCMP, Grogan was a "mole" who had been "sleeping" for twenty years before being activated to run this treasonous scheme. As the implications of this report sank in, the men of Metro Intelligence glanced nervously at one another, realizing that they alone were facing what was clearly the most serious

The secret band of ultra-wackos in the Investigative Support Services responsible for "Tailgate."

Commie threat to the province since the Attack of the Soviet Racoons had been repelled only the year before.

Intelligence Branch strategists were quickly brought in and soon devised several ingenious methods of countering this heinous Commie offensive. Their short-term tactic was to round up every single adult male in the province, and arrest anyone who could correctly pronounce the word "frijole."This plan had to be scrapped

when a team member spotted the Chief in a Taco Bell take-out line. As Intelligence plotted their next move, word came in on the five p.m. pigeon that the Grogan family was readying itself for a weekend drive in the Kawarthas. In fifteen frantic minutes, Operation Tailgate was formulated.

ISS Branch could think of no way to root out the Cuban agents directly, so they decided to put a "tail" on the Grogan family. This sudden and suspicious Grogan "vacation" gave the ISS the idea of trailing the family in disguise. The plan was to assemble a typical Ontario family, supply them with an unobtrusive car, and set them (figuratively) on the tailgate of the Grogan car.

Turning to their principle sociological reference work, the Sears catalogue, ISS strategists rounded up four agents from the Special Force to serve as their prototype family. And promptly ran into a snag.

No Metro Policeman is less than five feet, nine inches tall. It soon became obvious to the nonplussed operatives that even with appropriate makeup and costuming, no Metro cop could pass for a boy of eight and a girl of seven.

The problem was solved by calling in two members of the top secret OPP Playground Analysis Technical Surveillance Infiltration and Espionage

Squad — the dreaded PATSIES. Skilled in unarmed combat, with photographic memories, and an adult height of less than three feet, the PATSIES had been developed as a Secret Strike Force to off-set what the RCMP saw as an attempt by the agents of SCUM (Students Coalition to Undermine Motherhood), to recruit Commie operatives from the politically unsophisticated pre-school set in the playgrounds of Canada. The two PATSIES chosen were code-named Dick and Jane. Both were adult males, so lots were drawn to see who would wear the

sector benefactor remains unknown, it seems relevant to note that a famous hamburger chain was subsequently granted free space in the foyer of the headquarters building on Jarvis Street. However they did it, ISS men secured enough funds to purchase a used Vauxhall Victor, a tent-trailer, and a matching set of four Emergency Orange Snowmobile Suits. Code-named ''The Browns,'' the team at once set out on the trail of the Grogan spy ring, looking every inch the average Canadian family - circa 1962.

Toronto Police car

violet pinafore with the bunny motif and who would wear the grey flannel shorts and the blue beanie.

Since it looked like Operation Tailgate was going to exceed the $758 Contingency Fund the Intelligence Branch maintained for covert ops, the senior staff went to ''unnamed sources'' in the business community for more funds. While the identity of this private

To the incredulous delight of the control staff, ''The Browns'' soon reported visual contact with the Grogan station wagon on Highway 400 just south of Barrie. The Grogan vehicle, with Mr. and Mrs. Grogan in the front seat and the Grogan quadruplets in the back, were off on a ''suspiciously ordinary'' vacation. The ''Daddy'' of the surveillance team positioned the

Vauxhall a discreet distance behind the Grogan car and the jubilant operatives celebrated by passing out little plastic glasses of lime Kool-Aid and settling down to some serious espionage.

For the next twenty-four hours the Browns kept the Grogan family in constant contact, logging over 500 miles with only one vaguely suspicious incident. Stopping for gas at a Petro-Canada station in Bala, the Grogan quads spent what struck the police as an inordinate amount of time in the gas station washroom. The surveillance team quickly deduced that the quads might be contacting dangerous Cuban terrorists. Perhaps the quads were secret KGB agents assigned to leave hidden messages in service station washrooms across the province. With their blood running cold at the fiendish Commie cleverness of the scheme, the PATSIES rushed the door as soon as the quads left. But the only occupant of the room was an itinerant Lithuanian psychotherapist who attempted to resolve Agent Jane's ''obvious heterosexual rage'' before he was billy-clubbed to the terrazzo floor, and the chase resumed.

There was one other tense moment, when Agent Jane was dragooned into a game of double-jumpers by some blind children at a KOA Camp-ground near Fenelon Falls and skipped himself into a temporary coma. After that, Operation Tailgate proceeded without a hitch for another twelve hours.

On the evening of the second day, the dogged surveillance squad was cruising along behind the Grogan car

Map 1

Trendy's

Chow down at TRENDY'S, Toronto's first authentic rancho-style oyster palace. Enjoy these legendary aphrodisiacs with your choice of zesty toppings, including guacamole, bean curd and Texan road house chili. Expect to rub shoulders with screen greats, top Canadian politicos and Pierre Berton.

Attire required.

Yorkville Avenue

OLDE PIERRE'S YUKON CAFÉ

You are free to act like a Canadian in this informal pioneer stone farmhouse, located in historic Etobicoke. Built in 1957, this waterfront hideaway has been a Toronto dining tradition for more than 7 weeks. Thrill to Olde Pierre's dulcet tones as he reads from his menu. Cut an impressive figure as you languish in darkened rooms decorated with railroad memorabilia. VIA rail Toronto to Montreal timetable free with orders over $2.95.

Don Valley Parkway.
No reservation necessary.

KOSHER SZECHUAN TAKE-OUT

Yours to discover Jumbo lox with cherry sauce; sweet and sour matzo balls; anchovies served on small bamboo skewers.

No credit cards.
Spadina At Dundas
The Heart of Chinatown

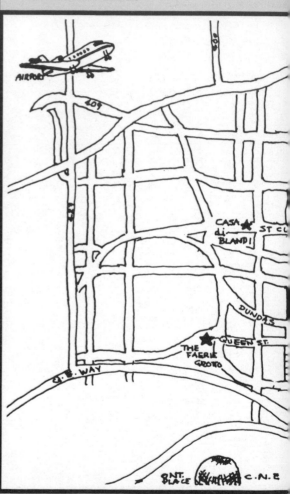

Casa di Blandi

Pietro Bertoni's family ristorante.
House wines from Spadina.
Real Wallpaper.

Corner St. Clair.

The Grogan Family assume "The Position"

thoroughly engrossed in a tense game of I Spy With My Little Eye. Suddenly the Grogan station wagon braked to avoid a suicidal ferret, and the undercover Vauxhall Victor punched into the back of the Grogan vehicle at roughly thirty miles an hour.

While no one was hurt in the collision, a fist-fight immediately broke out between Nigel Grogan and "Daddy Brown," who had taken a personal affront at being called a "noodle-necked chokecherry with the motor reflexes of a sloth." "Daddy Brown" immediately attempted to drag Grogan out of the car through a side-vent window. Mrs. Grogan, outraged, was coming to his defense when she was tripped and attacked by PATSIES Dick and Jane.

"Mommy Brown," who had kicked open his passenger door to clear the way for a leap into the fray, was sidelined when the door bounced off the hinge-spring and slammed back into his face. It was at this point that

the Grogan quads came piling out of the shattered rear window of the station wagon, dragged agents Dick and Jane off their mother and proceeded to batter the agents about the head and shoulders with their Star Wars light sabres. Agent Dick caught a very nasty one over the left eye and crumpled to the ground, leaving Agent Jane alone to deal with the now completely enraged Mrs. Grogan, who threw a very competent full-nelson on him and wrestled him to the dirt.

In a desperate attempt to salvage the operation, "Daddy Brown" broke away from Grogan and ran back to the ruined Vauxhall. He tore open the driver's door (which came off in his hand), reached under the dashboard and pulled out his Official Metro Police Officer's hat. Cramming it down over his ears, he ripped open the front of his kelly green Banlon golf shirt to reveal the Metro Police crest on his regulation T-shirt. He was in the process of arresting everyone within a sixty-mile radius when a Greyhound bus full of senior citizens returning from a lawn bowling tournament in Mount Albert ran right over him.

By passing off the incident as "just another unfortunate weekend traffic accident," ISS was able to keep this incredibly successful operation undercover. Every surviving member of Operation Tailgate was promoted to Sergeant and honoured with lifetime postings to the washroom patrols in the basement of Queen's Park. Shortly after the Postlethwaite Papers made headlines, everyone on the squad inherited large sums of money from "a sick relative in the Cotswolds," and left Canada.

So far, no sign of any Cuban terrorist offensive has developed, although anyone approaching the order desk of the Taco Bell restaurant on Dundas West in Etobicoke, and correctly pronouncing the word "frijole" will find himself followed home by a large green bush with six black feet.

Bush with six feet

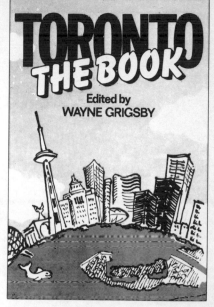

SPÉCIALITÉS OF THE DON VALLEY

From the wineyards of Ronnie Pasteur, three amusing new vintages!

From the Médiocre district, Yonge Gosling, a mildly perfumed sparkling white wine with just an after-hint of musk. This slightly sweet aromatic vintage was this year's winner of the coveted O'Keefe Golden Sauterne medal.
A classic at any table!

For beef, and other macho dishes, why not try Bordello, a rank and fulsome Italian-style vintage. This rich, sweet wine emits a hearty bouquet that belies its frankly cheeky flavour. Heart-warming and seductive, for any occasion.

For the more unconventional, why not serve Cold Turkey? Just add water to these spicy golden crystals, and you will have a plain-speaking madeira-like liquid that will leave guests astounded.

Mail orders accepted.
Free *'I drink with Ronnie'* stickers with orders of over a dozen.

In Defense of Toronto

Tina Srebotnjak

Let me spit out my prejudice right at the start. I love Toronto. Furthermore, I think Torontonians are nice people. Now I know such a bold assertion will have you fainting out there in the regions, but for once I'm going to put aside my quintessential Torontonian desire to be liked and give you guys the straight goods.

It's not very nice of you to keep maligning Toronto as you do, and frankly, it hurts. This is, after all, a terrific city. It just happens that through an accident of history and geography this is where the Canadian Big Time is. But frankly, is this our fault? *Some* place has to be the centre of the country, so why not Toronto?

After all, you could do worse. I mean, you could have Calgary. Aside from the thousands of aesthetic objections that leap to mind (which I'm far too well bred to enumerate here), just consider time zones. How would you people in Newfoundland like beginning your day in the middle of the afternoon? No, in a country as big as this one, Toronto seems the sensible choice.

Now I know you resent Bay Street. But it's really a rather innocuous little place. I mean there's hardly anyone *in* the street — they're all inside making the zillions of dollars that they send to Ottawa in equalization payments for the rest of the country. *Some* people might find a little gratitude appropriate here!

So, you don't like Toronto being the centre of things cultural. You have your own theatres and symphonies, but you still feel you have to come to Toronto in order to make it. Well, you don't. We've got quite enough unemployed actors and musicians; in fact, we could send you some. So if you want to stay in Saskatoon or Fredericton, we approve.

Now I know some of you have actually *been* to Toronto and that you've found the experience less than scintillating. You were, in fact, bored to tears. Frankly, this is one complaint I've never understood. How could one be bored in a city that has all these restaurants, theatres, cinemas, art galleries and bars?

Yes, yes, I can hear you saying, but it has no street life — no *joie de vivre*. You can't make eye contact with anyone in Toronto. Well, so what? I admit that Torontonians are a tad reserved, but why would you want to make eye contact with a total stranger, anyway? I mean, I don't want to make too big a deal of propriety, but you haven't even been introduced! As I see it, this bizarre desire to have dealings with people entirely unknown to you is your problem, not ours. You're probably the kind of person that creates a scene in restaurants too.

And just look how well behaved we are when it comes to the political scene. We all know, don't we, that Ontario has a big say in deciding which party wins federal elections. But once we send our refined ministers from Toronto to Ottawa, they don't exactly steal the headlines, do they? They don't fall all over themselves demanding new Post Offices or skyscrapers, or the immediate transfer of the Veterans' Affairs department to Willowdale. That's *noblesse oblige* for you.

You think us insensitive. Again, I beg to differ. No one tries harder to please than a Torontonian. We want you to like us. We want you to know that we care about the rest of the country — that we've actually heard of Salmonier, Newfoundland and Sooke, British Columbia. We're the first to admit, generosity bursting from our souls, that Vancouver is breathtaking; that Montreal is exciting; that there's lots of wheat in them there prairies. We even find Allan Fotheringham and Ray Guy mildly amusing.

If anything, Torontonians are the most compromising of Canadians. Why, you just tell us your vision of Canada and we'll adopt it as our own. We want desperately to do the right thing, to have the right opinion on issues near and dear to your hearts. I have given countless cross-cultural dinner parties myself, at which many of our provinces and even some of our territories have been represented. And I didn't mind doing it either, because that's the way Torontonians are.

So you can understand how inconsolable I become when all I ever hear rolling in from the regions are those nasty things you say about Toronto. Perhaps it's time you gave all this some thought.

We always say, here in the City, that you can talk anything out, and we're almost never wrong. Hasn't this little chat done us all some good? Don't you just want to reach out and hug a Torontonian? Aren't we, after all, just too cute for words?

TORONTO GRAFFITI

"Toronto places position over passion
but primarily prefers power
Witness Conrad Black
and the CN Tower."

HANA GARTNER

"We've just enlarged the store and put up a
new sign. It's the world's largest electrical
sign. It's 635 feet long by 30 feet high and
has 23,000 electric bulbs — all going at the
same time. It makes Las Vegas look like a
cemetary!"

HONEST ED MIRVISH

"Toronto is like a really good joke. You
have to be there to really enjoy it."

JAMIE WAYNE

"Real Torontonians wish they were living in
the City of North York."

MEL LASTMAN
Mayor of North York

"I left L.A. because of the bullshit. Toronto, basically, is just calf shit. The only fear I have about Toronto, a city which I adore, is that cows grow up."

LOUIS DEL GRANDE

"The Bible tells us that 'Babel' was a city whose people, the descendants of Noah, tried to build a tower to reach heaven, but were prevented from doing so by God, who punished the builders for presuming they could reach heaven by Tower. He caused them to speak different languages so that they could not understand one another. Toronto has its own 'Tower of Babel' . . . our very own CHIN Radio stations, speaking out, with love, in over 30 languages . . . all together at one time . . . and getting to understand each other better and better . . . and known to have heavenly connections!"

JOHNNY LOMBARDI
President CHIN Radio

"Real Torontonians are now gastonome; they eat at Gaston's."

GASTON SCHWALB
Gaston's Restaurant

"I was born in 'Toronto the Good,' and as it became less good — it got better!"

SAM SNIDERMAN
Sam The Record Man

METRO MISCREANTS

153792

BERNARD WIERD, SENTENCED
TO 350 YEARS MINUS A DAY
FOR MOVING INTO THE
BEACHES AREA OF EAST
TORONTO WITHOUT BEING
A MEMBER OF THE MEDIA.
HE LOST ALL CHANCE FOR
PAROLE, AFTER SERVING
139 YEARS, FOR FAILING
TO RECOGNIZE THE
PROMINENT BEACHER,
LARRY ZOLF.

97327

DAVID WIFFLE, SENTENCED
TO 5000 YEARS MINUS A
DAY FOR EMPLOYING A
SLINGSHOT AND PEBBLES
TO SINGLE-HANDEDLY AND
WANTONLY DESTROY THE
ENTIRE DOWNTOWN TORONTO
ARCHITECTURE. METRO
WORKS REQUIRED FOUR
WEEKS TO CLEAN UP
ACRES OF COATED AND
TINTED GLASS.

421735

WILY McBUBBLES,
SENTENCED TO
ETERNAL EXILE
OUTSIDE OF METRO
TORONTO FOR
SUGGESTING THAT
THE POSITION OF
METRO CHAIRMAN
BE WON BY PUBLIC
VOTE. IN HER DEFENCE,
SHE CLAIMED TO SPEAK
FOR ORDINARY
TORONTONIANS. THE
JUDGEMENT POINTED OUT
THAT THERE WERE NO
ORDINARY TORONTONIANS.
SHE WAS BANISHED TO
MISSISSAUGA, WHERE
PEOPLE ARE ORDINARY.

721531

ESTELLE LEPORC,
SENTENCED TO 897 YEARS
MINUS A DAY FOR
SUGGESTING A GAY PIG
AS A FITTING LOGO FOR
TORONTO, ONCE KNOWN AS
HOGTOWN. CITY OFFICIALS
ADDED ANOTHER 10,000
YEARS WHEN SHE
RESPONDED TO HER
SENTENCE BY CALLING
HER BETTERS, "SWINE."

Graham Pilsworth